Bringing Forth the Man

A Handbook for Single Moms Raising Teenage Boys

by

Richard V. Eastman
Founder of Self-EducationLAB

authorHOUSE

1663 Liberty Drive, Suite 200
Bloomington, Indiana 47403
(800) 839-8640
www.authorhouse.com

First published by AuthorHouse 12/12/05

ISBN: 1-4208-9528-1 (sc)
ISBN: 1-4208-9529-X (e)

Printed in the United States of America
Bloomington, Indiana

This book is printed on acid-free paper.

SUCCESSFUL STUDENTS MUST "LEARN TO THINK, ASK
QUESTIONS, ANALYZE PROBLEMS, FIND SOLUTIONS.
BE AN INDIVIDUAL AND BE CREATIVE."
Gerald Celente.
Trends 2000

THIS I BELIEVE

The condition of our schools and our communities are the
responsibility of old-timers like myself. We need to correct our
mistakes.

I also believe the thinking of Carl Rogers Ph.D.in "Freedom To
Learn", if correctly used, will accomplish more in one-hour, than
a full-day of traditional classes. It will improve results in all
other required classes.

INTRODUCTION FOR STUDENTS: A USER'S GUIDE TO LEARNING

At the age of fourteen my father and I had an argument. We rolled around on the floor and somehow I bloodied his nose. This was the most horrible day of my life. From then on my life changed; I moved into a boarding house in Billings, Montana. I worked across the street for Lew Chevrolet as a mechanics' helper and as a tow truck driver. This was during the second World War when every able-bodied man had been drafted. It was easy to get a job anywhere.

Two months later with all my belongings in a paper bag, I rode the Greyhound bus to Live Oak California to pick peaches. The rumor was that it was possible to make twenty dollars a day. I wanted to make money so I could attend a diesel mechanic school. I lived in the old Cottage Hotel until a weird old man down the hall came into my room to let me know that he loved me more than I loved myself. I was a scared kid at the age of fourteen and got out fast.

While working on a chicken ranch I found a friend, Bruce Dallas, who offered me a place to live. Some of the guys I worked with wanted me to play football at Live Oak High. So I decided to join them. This meant that if I was going back to school I had to find a way to live. I found a job working at Wilson Hardware. Mr. Wilson became my best friend; he treated me like his own son for five years. Of course I had to lie about my age to get the job. Farmers in the area used to kid me about being eighteen longer than anyone they had ever known.

After my second year in school, I woke up one morning crying. I had to see my dad and mother immediately. I could no longer live with my conscience. While still crying I went to work and told Mr. Wilson I had to go home. He offered me two weeks pay, but said I had to see my principal, Mr. Hendricks, for approval to leave school one month early. At noon that day I was on the train; a teenager on the road again, for the excitement of my life. On arrival I could not believe how kind and generous my father had become.

My education in elementary school ended halfway through the seventh grade when I went to work on the railroad with my dad. In Live Oak I attended high school for only three years. Two years later I graduated from Yuba College with an AA degree. I attended La Verne College and quit one science class short of a B.A. degree. I had my own ideas about what should be studied.

** **

The trash can of our society, a kind of hide-away for teenagers who think school is irrelevant, is the California Youth Authority. It's a sad place for children who are waiting for adults to teach them, rather than independently learning how to learn. I often wonder how many great leaders are stifled by the boredom of our schools. Winston Churchill was a good example. He was an adventurous soul who hated school. He believed there was no happiness without creative activity, self education, a "work" of some kind. He had many interests and hobbies.

As a youth counselor I have asked the question hundreds of times: why are you in jail? Not *what have you done*, but *where did you go wrong*? The most common answer was not drugs, family, or environment. The answer was, "I started going wrong in school and never stopped." Well, what went wrong in school? First of all, they felt like a nobody in the school setting. Have you ever felt alone in a crowd? Ask yourself how a mature adult would react to that kind of situation; few will tolerate just being a number on a time card; they want to be involved in their work. They often turn away, look for another job—not an option for a teenager bored with school!

Compare your own lot with that of an adult: at this point in your life you have less patience and more freedom than the average adult; fewer financial responsibilities, and no fear of change. But like any adult you want a certain amount of responsibility, want to put in your two-cents worth, want to be listened to, given respect, not be treated like the kid you were just a few years ago. You need more goals and fewer rules, to find out exactly what you can be, what you can learn to become and accomplish.

So how do you find those goals when school is boring and your teachers and parents don't listen? How do you make this time in your life a rewarding and fun experience and an adventure?

**

My most rewarding work experience was as a Group Supervisor and Youth Counselor with the California Youth Authority. This may sound unbelievable, given what I have written above. But I put my heart and soul in these kids. There were certainly many sad moments, but I learned the most about my fellow humans in this time, and how we relate to each other as students and teachers, as prisoners and prison-keepers. And sometimes the similarities were disturbing.

Many times I found they had returned to our institution—institutionalized—or with the comment, "Perhaps it is God's will." I hated these excuses. Too many also continued a life of crime.

Our in-service training focused on the best tool we had: listening. With tongue in cheek I gave myself the title, The World's Best Listener. No one ever questioned it. They just said countless times, "I don't believe it, Mr. E. really cares." And I did. I had been a teenager with an unusual experience. I had a great empathy for them. And I actually listened, which was something they were not used to, from their parents or teachers.

**

Over the years I have learned that to take control of one's life, you have to learn to become a leader. How do you learn to lead? Can a teacher teach you how to lead? No. Teachers and parents can assist in your becoming a leader by giving you some of the tools, and the time, to do it yourself. But one of the things leaders know is that the only way to get something you really need and want is to do it yourself. This book is one of the tools to help you do that.

This book tells you how to use one hour a day of your time to take control of your life. Some of the results of this will be immediately recognizable to you—you'll be more in control of your ability to communicate, you will have more confidence when you are confronted with finding out about new things, you'll have that rich sense of knowing things that others do not, you may even be able to share some of this knowledge as you learn. In the longer term, you will feel a stronger sense of self, and find yourself directed more surely to the things about which you really want to learn, that will help you in your journey through this life. You'll learn the importance of creating solitude for yourself to learn. You might even feel others looking up to you now and then because of these innate changes in yourself; then you will know that you are starting to become a leader.

How do you do this in an hour a day? The answer begins in Chapter Three. I have written the first two chapters for the most part for teachers and parents, because teachers and parents can help in this process, give you the freedom and tools you need to make this happen. In doing so, they can contribute to making schools better for all of us.

But you can also do it yourself; you don't need to wait for some kind of "program" to take charge of your life and your learning. It just takes a little willpower to get started, and then the feeling of discovery (and self-discovery) will propel you onto your own unique path toward leadership.

So if you want to read what I have to say to parents and teachers, feel free to read the Introduction for Parents and Teachers, and the first two chapters of the book. It may help, and it may be a little entertaining, too, to see how adults have to talk to each other in books to get a good idea rolling.

But if you want to start yourself, which any leader would want to do, jump right ahead to Chapter Three. And if you have any questions, ask your parent or teacher who has this book what they think; or, email me! My email is rich.eastman@gte.net and as I said before, I'm still the World's Best Listener.

Richard Eastman
June, 2002

INTRODUCTION FOR PARENTS AND TEACHERS

or, How to Be Famous in Your Own Home or School

This is an introduction that explains my research and experience with young people. It touches on three thousand years of wisdom from writers concerned with education of our youth. It expands on the thinking of Carl R. Rogers Ph.D., a great teacher of teachers who wrote *Freedom to Learn*. Years ago his thinking went through an experimental stage that failed because of one simple mistake. They thought that students could be given a full day of freedom to learn, at what would be an exciting pace. As it turned out students cannot make use of that much free time. They became students lost in space, the world was too big for them. Most of us know kids need discipline; they cannot live without it.

I believe, if your claim to fame is not "I am The World's Best Listener," then you are—in the eyes of a teenager—not famous. You have not become a role model. Every healthy teenager looks up-to the famous. They expect to be famous. You can, if you like, be famous in your own home.

"Nothing worth learning can be taught, it must be learned" was a Rogers theory. He also said, "a student who has been taught will forget what they have been taught almost immediately. But students who learn with their own interest and enthusiasm will keep what they have learned forever." Rogers believed the intensity and the speed of learning would be dramatic if students focused on learning the things they love. Also, if teachers help students learn what they want to learn, (Rogers called it facilitation.) the momentum established would accelerate learning.

Great thinkers in history are critical of today's teaching methods. Research makes it obvious Rogers' thinking came from several writers in history. If you look at the Education Quotations in this book you will find the thinking of 70 writers with 180 opinions. You will find these similarities surprising. Most of these quotations make it clear; learning is something we do for ourselves.

This book's main proposal is that if for one hour per day we make use of our natural desire for independence, this natural human curiosity, and this desire to learn, that we would go a long way towards solving some of the fundamental problems with our educational system; more importantly, we would be encouraging a new class of self-taught, highly motivated young people to engage the world directly and not cling to the failure of our educational systems as the reason for their own failures.

In a sense, we have been fighting a problem, all of these years, that is not even there. If we use what comes naturally, for just one hour a day, would that improve a teachers ability to help students learn? I think it would magnify the teacher's value many times. We have become controllers who listen only to ourselves, rather than listeners looking for a way to help a child find what they are good at. Instead of looking for genius, we stifle thousands of students everyday. Why is it we are so slow to learn? Simplicity, as usual, is the cure for most of our problems. One hour of focused freedom each day will dramatically change boredom into love for learning.

Our children feel like they are welfare recipients. They have no control, no credibility, and no way to add their thinking to the education process. They need to feel at least partially in control of their own learning. Where is the respect all children deserve a chance to prove they deserve?

"I feel smaller, weaker and less a person, learning, what others think I should learn. I am only obedient; driven by fear." I doubt this is what most of us want our children to think; but isn't that how we teach them?

The big question is: What should their direction be, where should they go? All they really know is they want to be independent. If there is work to do they want to do it without help. I like to suggest: find a word, usually a noun, and then spend one month learning all they can about this one word. (Courage is one of their favorite words.) I can assure you, after thirty-days, if they have been serious about their work, their life will never, again, be the same. For more favorite words and complete explanation see Chapter Two, Part One.

Managing: Time, Space, and Materials

A manager is a manager. He or she who can manage, can manage a service station, a farm, or a school. Managers use all natural possibilities. Two famous management consultants, Dr. Peter Drucker and Dr. W. Edwards Deming, have management theories that can be applied to our schools. If we combine their thinking with that of Dr. Carl R. Rogers, we have a formula that will improve learning in our schools and reduce the costs dramatically.

Dr. Drucker believes that to manage anything, the use of Time, Space, and Material must be defined, measured, and maximized. I think it's true that an Olympic runner must compete with herself if she expects to be her best. In other words, every minute of every day in the space you occupy should be productive; if not, you may be using the wrong tools or materials.

Dr. Deming has world-famous management theories that have been ignored by Civil Service Managers. His thinking is only common sense:

• Only managers can change the "us-against-them-attitude."

• Managers and employees are equally responsible for quality performance.

• Recognition and cooperation must be built into all management and employee relationships.

• Managers must help employees find a way to make changes which employees think necessary.

• A manager's most important work is commitment to the search for improvement.

• Failure, a lack of success, is most often caused by the system, not by an employee's work performance.

• If self-education is encouraged, employees will change, grow, and get better, in every area of their life; both at work and home.

• Employees must find joy and enthusiasm in their work. They can, if they help design the system they work in.

• Individualism can be honored when teams work to support each other.

The thinking of these three men can change mediocrity into excellence. One fact, strong leadership cannot deny: *"If you are not getting better results every year, poor management is the reason."*

Listen to the positive words of a responsible Master Teacher. "If the student has not learned, the teacher has not taught." Management theories suggest that teachers are not given the support they need to be successful. The increased strength of Teacher Unions supports the theory that management has not been a good listener. The excellence teachers want for their students has not been a management obsession.

To draw a blunt comparison based on my experience, the same is true with prison management. Increased union power has been dramatic because managers have not made employees a significant part of the management process. When management consultant suggestions are discussed with both school and prison administrators, the conclusion is their theories have no value. I am embarrassed with my thinking, but if I am honest, I could not disagree more. Most Civil Service managers do not understand the potential, the possibilities, and value of their work. They neglect a serious responsibility, even in their own communities.

We have been looking in the wrong place for answers. Part of my purpose for this book is to prove managers are either not open-minded, or looking in the wrong place for answers they honestly want. Education is more an art than a science, so the emotions, the gut feelings of the student can be used to improve the results of education. We are not listening. What is the problem?

We have not sold the idea—we have not convinced students—that we now have a quality and beneficial school system. If they are not convinced, a thousand words spoken by adults will not change their mind; they, like employees at a car factory with abusive management, will sabotage their own work to prove a point.

The relationship between buyer (student) and seller (teacher) must be recognized, and then honored. Any client who is buying a service needs the privilege of giving feedback, so together the buyer and seller can collaborate in their search for excellence. These are the natural events of any win/win situation.

Eskimos do not buy refrigerators; there is no need. How can a teacher sell education to a teenager if they are not convinced it will put money in their wallet? Our educational system is focused on the education of students who have a Mom and Daddy who will buy their first car. We have not made the sale because we have not yet listened to the needs of teenagers. Perhaps we talk too much; we like the sound of our own voices too much.

This thinking may sound childlike to the so-called elite authority, but like it or not when students become teenagers they begin to ask questions. They want answers and proof they are a significant person in projects that make a difference. They all want to be important, "somebody." Who can blame them? Don't we all want to be significant?

We are the source of our own education. My collection of famous quotations from three thousand years of history will explain the thinking of a great teacher of teachers, Dr. Carl Rogers Ph.D. I suggest if you seriously want quick information on how to teach your children, read no further—turn immediately to the collection of quotations on education. If we study and think about these quotations we will discover *most people are the source of their own learning.*

If students are given the time to use Dr. Carl Rogers' thinking they will develop the habit of learning on their own. The self-respect they gain and their ability to study without help will increase their enjoyment of learning. This includes subjects, again, which so-called experts think students must study. Samuel Johnson has a useful thought for experts. He said, "When you put on your pants it makes no difference which leg you put in first. While you are trying to make up your mind, sir, your backside is bare." Flexible thinking and opportunity to be creative will help students find new hobbies, new interests, new subjects they enjoy learning; without, incidentally, being forced into a box they are not yet ready for.

**

It is my opinion that humans are largely what they make of themselves; in other words, "human nature" is not much an empirical reality as a process of self-construction. This means that if people become what they think they are, what they think they are is exceedingly important.
—*Linda Marie Fedigan*
The Sun, *Jan. 2001*

**

One Hour a Day

One hour per day is all a student needs. Students learn how to act, or how not to act, from examples adults set for them. Our youth deserve more credit than most of us give them. They can't be fooled; they know both good and bad teachers when they see them. The first day that controlling teachers discover they are not as important as they think they are will be the first day that children will take on the responsibility for their own learning. This statement will cause many teachers to be outraged, I suggest if you are wearing a shoe that does not fit, you have even more problems than you realize. If we listen to teenagers we will find they are impatient with nonproductive busy work. When they find confidence from work they have done with their own hands, they will learn from both good and bad teachers. Responsibility for their own learning will drive them relentlessly forward. Education will become their own invention. This can be done in the first hour of their school day. As adults, most of us will agree that there is nothing like pride of ownership; so how could we not encourage self-designed learning?

We can no longer ignore the great writers and thinkers who have proven they have learned how to learn. These writers understand a truth that cannot be denied…the nature of children has not changed. The process of learning has not changed. The process of educational systems has changed, and that change has had sometimes disastrous results.

Learning Is: Desire, Enthusiasm, Expectation, and Excitement. An important book finds a way to focus on these words: *Mentally Tough* by Dr. James E. Loehr and Peter J. McLaughlin explains the learning success of Olympic athletes who take home the gold medals. This is about learning to focus on small parts of the larger process, and about learning successful habits. Examination of this information will help us to see the value of leadership. Sometimes, a good coach is all we are missing. Coaches don't play the game; they help the players improve and sharpen their skills and performance as individuals and a team. Teachers have the same job.

Lack of leadership is a problem in both schools and prisons. It is clear, if you listen to the many experts that each has a different solution. There is no positive direction. We are like a football team with several coaches, or like restless shoppers milling about, confused, under a swap-meet tent. We must constantly remind ourselves (every hour if necessary) that three words measure our work. They are: time, space, and material. If any one of these words become out of balance the job is not getting done. Experiment with this concept; you will eventually begin to believe it. I suggest do not surround yourself with busy work. It must be delegated, so the focus on constant improvement is an hour by hour obsession. Strong leaders are not timid, they have a relentless desire to serve and focus on excellence.

Like most administrators, school and prison administrators are not creative. Managers of schools and prisons appear to have no "fire in the belly," no "service to client" obsession. They are Civil Service employees who are not providing leadership. (Part of the problem is that politicians make demands that have no value.) On the spot managers need to take a risk, make a decision, and act courageously on their own ideas. Also, they need to get over the foolish idea that every decision they make has to be correct. Fear of looking bad or being embarrassed with decisions cannot be tolerated in the modern world of management. Lower-level managers should have the ability to manage their own time, space, and material. Their decisions should continuously improve with results that can be measured.

The macho male leader with simplistic answers has died and gone to heaven. Managers can no longer hide behind the security of unions. Because of this they need to bury themselves in leadership literature if they expect excellence from their employees. If they cannot learn to help employees improve the work managers want, learn to teach, and learn to motivate, they should be demoted to a less important job. As Truman said, "The buck stops here." Ted Turner has a favorite quotation, "Lead, follow, or get out of the way."

**

Education and Crime

The first day that the macho-male decides that he does not have all the answers, and the first day he decides he can improve his habits is the first day he can look in the mirror and truly see what kind of person he has become. If he discovers and believes it's true "that no man is an island," the world of discovery immediately opens up. This means that the only limit he puts on himself depends on the measure of courage he has to make mistakes, and still live with love in his heart.

Education and crime are related. Crime is a real problem we must deal with. It is not safe to walk the streets at night because crime has reduced us to mere puppets in our homes. Again we have many excuses but no one clear reason. When this foolish debate is over, education will reduce our problems to ten words or less. *We have forgotten the power of education.* If we try to separate education from crime we are separating identical twins that cannot deny each other. Crime in the United States can be prevented with schools that "work."

Likewise, an academic atmosphere will improve jailhouse mentality. Very important: taxpayers should not pay one thin dime for inmate education. If inmates want freedom it is their responsibility to work, work, work, at least eight hours a day like you and I must work. There is no free lunch; they must show interest in and evidence of change.

A controlled institution is a failure every time. In other words if the "boss" does all the thinking you can expect failure. It seems to me every prison in America is over managed by noncreative controllers who to want control. Having physical control makes their job easy. Changing attitudes and thinking has not been a part of their expertise; their biggest job, however, is to change people. Self-education should be the most important prison activity. A focus on self-education will change thinking, reduce management problems, and costs dramatically. Carl Rogers' learning process could have changed inmate education and prison results if he had been given the opportunity.

Supply and Demand:
Our Prisons Supply Crime & Criminals

Prisons are the largest wholesale supplier of crime in America. Prisons promote negative thinking, and all other bad habits that a human being can have. Our prisons are the largest single manageable, yet unmanaged, wholesale suppliers of crime in America. Prison managers have not been careful whom they associate with, so their thinking has become very much like their environment.

If they don't look for change and possibilities, they will find none. Prison managers should insist on self-education. Inmates should know education is the road to success. There are no excuses. I see only confusion; few have a goal of any kind. Truly, lack of inmate education has been the cause of failure and deeply affects our way of living. The answer to our problem is simple.

Make a learning atmosphere mandatory; a necessary part of jail time. Let all inmates work together to raise the level of education. Most people don't realize inmates love being the master of their own destiny; they are anxious to learn. We can provide material, "with feedback from them," which will raise their level of their thinking, their level of education.

Courage creates results while fear becomes failure. We as a society need to convince ourselves, and really believe it; "there is a solution to every problem." Some may say I have no sympathy for victims. Not true. I have a great deal of sympathy. But, we need higher expectations; let's solve the problem so we have less people getting hurt. We have to ask the question, why are we feeling sorry for ourselves? Why are we acting like a people who don't know how to solve problems? Where is the leader around this campfire?

My mission is to improve our schools and reduce crime in America:
- By renewing interest in Leadership
- By focusing on the real problem... Education
- By helping crime's nearest relative... Education
- By focusing on an unchallenged source of crime... Prisons

This will in my opinion give self-respect back to students and save taxpayers millions of dollars.

What This Book is For

We all know a better community depends on the education of our youth. This book is a perfect example of what every individual and every community in America should focus on. Our goals and expectations should shoot for the stars; they should be higher than anything we have ever experienced. I believe every community can rise to a higher level with leaders who have the courage too call the right plays. If they are right fifty-one percent of the time the communities win.

The problem is we tolerate mediocrity from those who affect our life the most. These people are our want-to-be-leaders. They are Civil Service Managers in both our schools and our prisons. The truth is these managers do not understand results; they do not see the potential, the value of their work.

Our schools should help students "learn how to learn."

Our prisons should not release parolees until they are ready for their communities.

This book, like any individual or community, is not as good today as it can eventually be. I am absolutely sure of one thing: my writing and thinking will improve as I learn from my mistakes and make changes that work. This can only happen if I have listened to you. Our community institutions should also change, grow, and get better each day in the same way. They will not improve unless we have the courage to go for the Gold. The truth is, while striving for excellence we will make mistakes, but if we are not making mistakes we are not trying hard enough.

Mistakes are not mistakes. Mistakes should not be considered the end of the world; they are the beginning of a new and better world. They are the source of all experience, understanding, all learning. It seems obvious, we need to create a history of both good or bad experience to learn from. Without courage we will continue making the same mistakes year after year. Thomas Edison and many others set examples we must imitate: each failure is another opportunity. If understanding the word *leadership* is not important in our life it should be; we are all imitated leaders everyday in some way.

Leadership should be the first scheduled class in every high school. No class is more important than attitude toward yourself and others. Someone said, "Insanity is doing the same thing over and over expecting different results." Bookstores and libraries have entire sections filled with books on Leadership, yet both state and federal managers totally ignore this information. The one thread that runs through most of these books are three words: Listening, risk and action. They need to take a risk on the value of their own thinking. They need the courage do whatever works until something better is found. Their obsession should be, "constant improvement" in the use of time, space, and material.

It's a mental thing, an attitude: This book will serve its purpose if we all begin to realize our lives and communities can improve when we truly believe it's possible. It's an expectation we must adopt. Why are taxpayers not more demanding? Why don't we adopt the idea that every problem has a solution? Truly if we lack confidence, if we don't think we can improve our communities, you can be sure that we will not…it's that simple!

We have developed the beginning of what I hope will be a seed-for-change: this book is a source of both practical and inspirational information teenagers can use to create self-designed self-respect. Students will learn to respect *the value of their own thinking* when they have learned to focus on what they like best. The result will be ownership, "his or her own invention."

TABLE OF CONTENTS

CHAPTER 1

Parents

Experts Do Not See the Whole Picture

In hundreds of group sessions with young men, I have heard the expression, "Tell us where you are coming from." This often means: who are you? I am luckier than most people; I have spent most of my life with young people. Here is part of my story. I left my home at the age of fourteen and later returned only for vacations. I have been classified, qualified, and certified: a juvenile delinquent. Loneliness followed me everywhere I found myself; but solitude was in my favor. It gave me time to think about real problems. Because of my experience, teenagers have a special place in my heart. My focus in life eventually became the problems of young people. I have always felt that I care more than most people. It's probably not true, but true or not, it has been important for me to put myself in the shoes of young people. It's the only way I know how to increase my chance of helping them.

If there is such a thing as a sixth sense, a better understanding of teenage problems, I believe I have as much or more than most people. I am often amused, but mostly disappointed with the experts who think they know how to solve the problems of our youth. It often seems these experts, who ever they may be, have never been teenagers themselves, or have conveniently forgotten that period in their lives.

Many had no solitude or opportunity to live the experience fully. They were too busy with their own experience to see the big picture. Many of the experts have a frustrated desire to control and impose their thinking on a youngster who it seems is easy to dominate. Many have made their opinionated decisions without the honesty of discussion. Their thinking needs a good challenge.

If they had a sailboat in the ocean with a gentle breeze they would do just fine. But, the stormy life of a teenager does not respond to the usual adult fear or control. Teenagers who are trying hard to be their own person are not sympathetic with adults who don't understand. They consider themselves tough and capable, yet they are begging for strength to lean on. They want us to show them their potential, but they want to find their own way.

Sometimes it is more effective to go with the natural flow of the storm rather than fight every emotional wave, plus the wind and rain. The best coaching is done from the sidelines. For the sake of teenagers, I pray we adults will do less teaching and more coaching. The difference is amazing.

Don't Read Books on Parenting—Read Books on Leadership

Parenting books can be helpful in many ways, but leadership allows us to see the forest from the top of the highest tree. Interest in leadership will take you places you have never been before. It's the higher plane of teaching rather than preaching. A teenager's need is someone who will watch them perform and catch them just before they break their leg.

If as parents we find that we need to brag about being leaders, or let our children know we are the leader, then we are not their leader—we are their controller. Who needs a controller when you feel like crying?

What is a leader? A leader helps set a course and facilitates constant changes in the endless process of learning.

As parents and teachers we cannot play the game of life for them. Our job is to follow where they want to go by leading them, without controlling them. Leaders who have a quiet faith and confidence do not expect a pat on the back; they give students credit for their own success. Leadership is our responsibility so we need to be patient, yet passionate about good manners, and respect for others. Our good examples are always the best teachers. Albert Schweitzer believed, "Example is not the main thing in influencing others. It is the only thing."

There are as many kinds of leaders as there are people. Our own style, whatever works, clearly explains what kind of person we have become. A good coach has to have had the experience of playing the game with unusual effort. This includes honesty, integrity, and the desire to help others achieve goals. "Man" is not an island in himself; so a father, mother or teacher must share their experience openly. Most often we can all learn together and from each other.

All Readers are not Necessarily Leaders, but All Leaders are Readers.

What is wrong with all of us feeling like we are leaders? Would that simple thought take us to the higher-level of a great parent and a great teacher? I think so. For years I have told my six boys and one girl that I am the world's best driver. I'm probably not, but who cares? I am a better driver because of thinking I am, and trying every day to prove to myself and my children that I am.

I love books. I love reading, learning, and searching for truth. One of my favorite subjects has been the leaders of the world since the beginning of time. There is no such thing as a successful leader who has not been obsessed with excellence in some form.

Thomas Edison is a good example of a man who wanted to learn by searching for information found in books. His curiosity led to what has or has not worked. He knew that mistakes are the source of most learning and eventual wisdom. He knew mistakes made by others would help him. Leaders must have the courage to make mistakes. He made over ten thousand mistakes to create the light bulb. Ten thousand mistakes! This is especially interesting when you consider that the symbol for a great idea is usually a light-bulb going on over a person's head. That light-bulb didn't go on without trial and error.

I'm convinced all parents must accept the fact, like it or not, that they are leaders. A parent's main job is to lead. If children are important, then leadership is important. The qualities of effective leadership must be a constant study. All parents should take a serious interest in what makes a good leader. The qualities of strong leadership are many, but one that cannot be ignored is *self-education*. Successful parenting is not an accident. It is more like an educated guess or simulating a trip to the moon—knowing that you have to estimate making a unique trip that nobody has made before, and that you may be off course ninety percent of the time.

But a change of course is a constant need in daily life. I believe every home in America should have books that teach leadership. Parents are truly flying by the seat of their pants without leadership skills.

Shouldn't leadership be the first High School class? Teenagers, even in their state of uncertainty, often have a great confidence. They have more courage than adults because they have not yet been beaten down by their inability to solve problems. Life has not yet happened to them: it has not become dull, their first love is still there, no dreams have soured, no friends have moved on, no death has changed who they are, Mom and Dad have not given up. The alligators of life do not yet surround them. How sweet it is. "If only my parents could see things as they really are," they often think. And to an extent they do not realize, they are right!

Teenagers think there is a solution to every problem. I preach and teach that every problem has a solution. I'm obsessed with this thought and when I get teenagers in a group, they can see I believe it. Most problems, reduced to ten words or less, can be handled with ease. I believe this, *but mistakes are allowed.* I can think of no reason to be anything but optimistic. I teach optimism in every way I can think of. Hope is a driving force that allows us to take a risk on our own thinking, make mistakes, and still learn something new every day. Life without hope drives us into a corner that is bigger than both of us. Hope helps us run when walking seems the only possibility.

Hope is itself a species of happiness, and, perhaps, the chief happiness which this world affords.
—*Samuel Johnson*

Surviving and Arriving

This book is about surviving and arriving where teenagers want to be. It's about freedom for growth inside the perimeter of rules teenagers expect and appreciate. "Rules are Love in disguise." Young people instinctively know this. They test these rules often just to make sure we are still there in case they need us. They don't understand why we don't understand the pain they are feeling. Growth without knowing what you are "growing into" is scary. They want, most of all, to know that we are listening to them and their needs, not just the creaking of our own bones. Their most asked question is, "Why are adults not listening?"

My years of listening could help those who don't have time to listen or are not sure what to do next. I suggest that young people like young colts need a pasture to run in so they can discover confidence and learn to trust themselves. They desperately want to show Mom, Dad, and Teachers how fast they can run.

Learning in our schools is as important to students as work is to adults, who find work important. But like all adults, they want to be more than just numbers who dutifully punch the time clock. Students, very much like adults, think about their jobs twenty-four hours a day. If they go to this much trouble they expect to put in their two-cents worth, whether the boss likes it or not. To them there is no doubt, adults are the boss, but they have no fear, no rent to pay, no faces to feed, no shoes to buy.

Do you know anyone, who has confidence, who does *not* think they would be a better boss than the one they have? Do you know a teenager who does *not* think they would be a better parent than the one they have; at least part of the time? I would not want my children to be any other way. I can handle a kick in the shins everyday, if necessary. Our children do not need to be obedient slaves. They need to be strong confident children who have courage. Teenagers must be open to new experience without unnecessary fear of their own little world.

If they have the kind of spunk we want them to have, they will and do speak up, often in strange ways we do not expect. If the parents are naive or not up to the test they will be given, children will sabotage the family program. Sometimes they attempt to conquer the parents by dividing them. Being a mom and dad of a teenager requires patience, but most parents will find that the mistakes they make or the problems they have can be solved with love...lots of love! Schools, however, are another subject outside this circle of love.

I believe our schools for teenagers are like prisons. Teenagers slowly die while still breathing because they are not able to be creative. They have no focus, no passion, and no obsession that drives them relentlessly forward. Instead they are like puppets just doing what they are told. They are bored with their work because, like any good employee, they know there is a better way. However, they have no power, no credibility and they don't know how to invent another way! They might as well put a sign on their backpack, "I'd rather be golfing."

Parents Are Their Own Worst Enemies

Part of the problem is that too many parents are disappointed in themselves. Too many think they are a failure because they have no college degree. How can they pass on to their children, faith, hope, and a quiet confidence? Not enough parents realize what they have accomplished.

They begin to have second thoughts about their parenting skills. If they have done a good job with their children, they are not aware of it. There is an unnecessary pessimism in the air. They see only today's problems, not tomorrow's possibilities. Pessimism creates a fear their children will not do as well as they can.

Fear creates the need to control. Too much control reduces children to mere puppets who follow the same footsteps their parents have taken. The student's own special talent, which is entirely different from that of the parents, is often buried in fear and mediocrity.

My advice for parents is to walk and talk with confidence; know that someday we will have all of the knowledge we need. Our experience and the knowledge we find along the way will create a wisdom that is truly our own. Do everything we can to convince our children they will be learning how to learn every day of their life. True happiness is learning something useful that can be passed on to family and friends without expectations or repayment.

Remember that control we give our children is control we will have to give for a long, long time. If we help them learn self-discipline we give them a tool that will help them learn to manage themselves.

Self-discipline is nothing but a book of recipes or a book of football plays that make it possible for a student to learn how to solve one of life's problems. If our attitude clearly shows that there is "a solution to every problem," we will later find that our grandchildren are absolutely beautiful. That makes sense but we'll never know unless we try it!

We should not allow learning to be an accident, but let it be our intention. As a learning experiment with ourselves, let us focus on a word we have an interest in for one month. Since this is part of what we are offering students, let's do it ourselves. When we feel reasonably happy with our knowledge of that word we'll move on to another. We'll return many times to our first words and we will enjoy the changes we see in ourselves. Twelve words a year will change who we see in the mirror, guaranteed. We will have earned a graduate degree in reality.

How determined should we be to be a good parent?

Wisdom is to bare all, cheerfully
—author unknown

CHAPTER 2

Education (pt1)

Excellence in Education is Like a Game of Golf

(This is possibility thinking for an ideal one hour class of self-designed education.)

What is the difference between golf and school? Golf allows freedom to make your own mistakes. A player can kick himself or herself for failure, and then, practice with renewed enthusiasm. They have fun working where they see the need for improvement. The decisions they make, without help, help them decide what they need to learn next.

They work at their own pace as hard and often as they want. They can eat, drink and sleep with it, twenty-four hours if they like. They use visualization to achieve a goal: the perfect work, a shot that is sweet, a judgment call that is right on.

"Was that luck, or am I getting the feel for the game?" They choose and they focus on that part of their work they think needs improvement. They decide if and what criticism, correction, or advice they want to use. Students have the privilege of asking for coaching. They also choose one or several coaches who they think will satisfy their needs. They love to ask questions about their "work." No one preaches to them.

To be a genius is okay, but this is not a requirement for enjoyment or fulfillment; just the activity, the process, the pleasure of learning is fun. We may if we like, lie about our score, but there is no reason to do so. We have no need to pretend or impress adults in our life. Our only need is to satisfy ourselves. We can be honest. (This is where integrity is found.)

There is no need for manipulation that will fool parents into thinking we are learning. Pleasing parents is not part of the game. It's easy to see we are improving, our history of mistakes make us smile. We have freedom, above all things; to be as good as we want to be. The joy of being able to make our own decisions is motivational. Teenager thinking is: "Who would not want to push hard against the old way of doing things; there must be a better way." They think, "If I can do this my way, that is what I am going to do."

Writing is a safe way for students to make mistakes. They must, if they want to grow, find a way to make mistakes. If we try to stop them, they miss the chance to learn on their own. They want to be actively involved and responsible while growing, changing and getting better. Responsibility has a way of taking people out of that "I need to be taken care of" mentality.

Responsibility is a special kind of freedom. It has a maturing effect on young people who might say, "I know where I'm going and why." It takes away the shame of being a "kept person." It is so important that adults keep shame out of a teenager's life. Give them respect.

Children are not born with courtesy and good manners

Golf course courtesy and good manners did not evolve from hard and fast rules established one hundred years ago. Courtesy and good manners grew from the desire to learn and the freedom to create its own environment. Rules that work evolve not from fearful small-minded people who wish to control, but from people who have faith in people. They evolved from the need for respect for each other and respect for a quiet environment where thinking is possible.

There is a natural law that says: "Treat others the way you want to be treated." We've seen it taught as an important element in various religions across the centuries, from pantheism to Christinaity's Golden Rule. Courtesy and good manners evolved from thoughtful people who knew that written and unwritten rules of conduct are necessary. All advanced cultures have some form of the Golden Rule, which states the obvious but is not formulaic, allowing room for the individual to adopt the rule at any period of their life.

Excellence is not achieved overnight. It is achieved first of all because that is what parents want. Parents are the head coaches and we all know how important a good coach is. It is also accomplished by improving on history. A school manager's most important work is to see that improvement is made in activities every year.

Our children need the privilege of playing their own game one hour of each day. I am convinced over-management is the cause of talent going to waste and also the reason personal growth is reduced to mediocrity rather than excellence. Management gets what it discreetly checks on. But, we can't make the mistake of thinking rules are not necessary.

Rules are a guarantee that love is still there. Freedom is focused on this one simple word. It will stretch the brain to new ways of thinking and a faster way of learning.

The feeling of individual helplessness is a great and growing problem. But there is an answer. It is not very complicated Each person has inside him a basic decency and goodness. If he listens to it and acts on it, he is giving a great deal of what it is the world most needs. But, it takes courage.
—Albert Schweitzer

Many people are now trying to get more in control of their lives. Personally and politically they are concerned with both education and crime. They are worried about themselves and their children. The daily news, which is focused on education and crime, makes them worried more than ever. Because this is so important, I offer my experience to all who would like a different point of view. Education and crime are, in my opinion very much like identical twins. One cannot deny the other. *Education is the source and the result of most good or bad community activities.*

Our world is changing faster today than it has since the beginning of time. Keeping up with the world is a constant search for a balance that makes sense. Science with the aid of computers may have our children vacationing in outer space before long. But science cannot solve the emotional problems young people have. This makes it necessary for us to learn, change and grow in every possible way. Peace on earth will not be scientific.

I'm sure you will agree peace begins within. Education is critical. We need to learn to manage ourselves. Learning at the speed of a computer would be ideal. But as you will see, Bill Gates and Dr. Peter Drucker believe we all learn in different ways. My own approach to learning is without a teacher. I do this not because I have a problem with teachers. There are many good teachers and some are very special. Teachers are finding it difficult to do what they love doing. There will never ever be enough good teachers. Learning is our job, and our responsibility; so we need to search for teachers who fit our needs. There are times when the best teacher is a well-written book. The education of many famous people proves this point.

There are times when the only teacher we get is the one assigned to us, but that is not all bad. We can and should make an effort to learn from every person we come face to face with. Everyone is potentially a wise loyal advisor. We can learn from all people. It's a matter of attitude.

Remember that old saying, "Don't wait for your ship to comes in, swim out to it?" The chances are one billion to one that no other student has the same needs as you or I may have. No one can take care of us, like we can take care of ourselves. We should search for this special talent, the ones only we have been given and use them in every possible way. Two of my favorite quotations you may enjoy:

> *No one-not your parents,*
> *nor your teacher,*
> *nor your peers-*
> *can teach you,*
> *how to be yourself.*
> *—Warren Bennis*

> *Men are polished*
> *through act and speech.*
> *Each by each,*
> *as pebbles are smoothed on the*
> *rolling beach.*
> *With years a richer life begins,*
> *The spirit mellows.*
> *Ripe age gives tone to violins,*
> *Wine, and good fellows.*
> *—John T. Trowbridge.*

CHAPTER 3

Education (pt 2)

Problem Solving Made Easy

For years now, I don't know where I picked up the habit, I catch myself saying: "A quiet faith and confidence."

And, "Every problem has a solution."

A Quiet Faith and Confidence

A quiet faith and confidence sounds good; its a kind of nice way to live our life. I consider it my philosophy for living: the ultimate goal is to live quietly, with faith, and confidence.

If I have a problem I focus on one simple word, and then I learn all I can about the word. For instance, what am I saying and what do I mean when I say, "quiet faith and confidence?" The first thing I do is look up the words in the dictionary, then Roget's Thesaurus and a favorite book of quotations.

Here is my research on these three words.

(1) Definitions and Descriptions of Quiet

Descriptions from the dictionary and thesaurus: Without shouting, screaming, or trying to jump out of my skin. Gentleness,

15

moderation, sobriety, tranquility, tolerance, patience, calmness, unhurried, nonviolent, placid, cool, steady, serene, keep the peace, even temper, tranquil mind, command of temper, presence of mind, check oneself, master one's feelings, level headed, easy going, take one's time, at ease, mental calmness, self-assured, harmony, quiet life, untroubled, etc.

Quotations of Quiet

The good and the wise lead quiet lives.
—Euripides.

To have a quiet mind is to possess one's mind wholly; to have a calm spirit is to command one's self.
—Hamilton Wright Mabie.

If thou desire to be held wise, be so wise as to hold thy tongue.
—Francis Quarles.

Reserve is the truest expression of respect toward those who are it objects.
—Thomas De Quincey

Modesty is a shining light; it prepares the mind to receive knowledge, and the heart for truth.
—Francois Pierre Guizot.

Sense shines with a double lustre when set in humility.
—William Penn.

Willingness to be taught what we do not know is the sure pledge of growth both in knowledge and wisdom.
—Hugh Blair.

A docile disposition will, with application, surmount every difficulty.
—Manilius.

It is the docile who achieve the most impossible things in this world.
—Sir Rabindranath Tagore.

(2) Definitions and Descriptions of Faith
Descriptions from the dictionary and thesaurus: Trust, conviction, certainty, conception, thinking, impression, conclusion, a way of thinking, well founded, firm, settled, fixed, rooted, deep-rooted, unshaken, steadfast, calm, sober, dispassionate, belief, believe, take for granted, satisfy oneself, take one's word for, rely upon, confidence in, embrace, etc.

Quotations of Faith
You may be deceived if you trust too much, but you will live in torment if you do not trust enough.
—Frank Crane.

The only known cure for fear is faith.
—Lena Kellogg Sadler.

What I admire in Columbus is not his having discovered a world, but his having gone to search for it on the faith of an opinion.
—Anne Robert Jacques Turgot.

Faith is courage; it is creative while despair is always destructive.
—David Saville Muzzey.

The man who trusts men will make fewer mistakes than he who distrusts them.
—Conte Camillo Benso di Cavour

(3) Definitions and Descriptions of Confidence

From the dictionary and thesaurus: sure of oneself, inclined to trust, assured, certain, self-possession, in control, control one's feelings, feeling certain, belief in one's own ability, reliance on one's own powers, someone or something to be trusted, assurance, self-sufficiency, expectation, judgment, mental acceptance of something, an opinion, without doubt, suppose, expect, assume, take the bull by the horns, courage, boldness, to take a risk, create action, fearless, not timid, strong minded, buoyancy, optimism, enthusiasm, golden dreams, presume, promise oneself, etc.

Quotations of Confidence

The trust which we put in ourselves causes us to feel trust in others.
—Duc Francois de La Rochefoucauld.

Woe to the man whose heart has not learned while young to hope, to love—and to put his trust in life.
—Joseph Conrad.

That man who has inspired confidence in another has never lost anything in this world.
—Mahatma Gandhi.

Self-trust is the essence of heroism.
—Ralph Waldo Emerson.

Nothing in life is to be feared. It is only to be understood.
—Marie Curie.

You gain strength, courage and confidence by every experience in which you really stop to look fear in the face...You must do the thing which you think you cannot do.
—Eleanor Roosevelt.

Write your own mini-essay on what confidence means to you today. Having quiet faith and confidence is a philosophy of life. It can be a way of living and being who we want to be. It is expecting adventure in the many things we can do in our lifetime; knowing we can do it, and then having the courage to do it. Tiny steps may be only the beginning but confidence has a relentless way of reaching goals, and finding the special ability we all have; each in a different way.

Every Problem Has a Solution

Every problem has a solution is an optimistic way of saying, "I can take care of business." To believe it is possible should be in every situation the most important goal. A goal without a believer has no value, no reason, no purpose.

Crime is a problem that needs attention; let's see if we can solve the problem on paper. If we can truly define and state the problem it will solve itself. Do you believe that?

Let's see what we can do. There are three basic reasons for crime in America. They are in this order of importance: (1) Schools, (2) drugs, (3) prisons. The first, the quickest, the least expensive, doable, manageable, effective way to reduce crime is to focus on improving the prison system.

Prisons must correct what our schools have not done.

Our schools lost the interest of students who had the same goals as teachers because leadership did not give teachers the support they needed. (This I believe, I hope you will also.)

If the fun and adventure of learning in school had been instilled in our children, drugs would have been of little or no importance. Drugs would have been only a teenager's adventure, an attempt to break away from Mom and Dad, and become "my own person." Strong happy children have no time for drugs. Every thinking teenager with a quiet faith and confidence wants to make their own decisions. They must grow up, and only they can create this older, mature person. This has always been true and always will be true. Confident children want to be an important part of the world they are going to live in. If we don't believe this, if we don't have faith in them, we are all in trouble.

The Rousseau Institute makes use of the pupil's pleasure in personal activity, rather than reducing him to the passive role of a well-behaved and rather inattentive listener.
—*Paul Tournier*

Let's begin using Dr. Peter Drucker's approach for excellent management. He has a leadership quotation that works in all situations. For excellence: "We must maximize Time, Space, and Material." In other words, while working, every minute of every day, in the space you occupy, you should be productive; if not you do not have the tools or material to do the job.

TIME

If we find a way to make better use of time, will prisons be effective? If inmates learn how to manage time while working will they have more pride, more self-respect? Anyone who has been on welfare can verify this is a truth.

An ideal goal for a prison setting is Self-Education. I believe if there is no peace, and no learning in our prisons, crime will continue unnecessarily high. (If it is possible to convince anyone this is true, this is what I am attempting to do.)

Time management must be maximized in every possible way. It's very simple. If we breakdown each ten hour day into fifteen minute periods we will find small periods of time are manageable. Any problem in life reduced to a smaller size can be managed. Now is a good time to ask the question, how important is the use of time? For the mind-boggling shock of a lifetime, every taxpayer should have the experience of one-hour in a prison setting.

Absolutely nothing productive is being done with time. If the ordinary taxpayer used time in this way at work, they would be fired immediately. Why should inmates loaf while we must hustle all day, every day? Without work they have no pride in themselves.

Let's take a step back here and approach this as a one hour exercise. To make the meaning of time more valuable let's consult the dictionary and thesaurus.

Definitions and Descriptions of Time

Time is a period or occasion with reference to one's personal reaction to it. A period of existence, a term of apprenticeship, a term of imprisonment, a period or periods necessary, sufficient, or available for something, an allotted period during which something is done, a period worked or to be worked by an employee, a rate of speed in marching, driving, working, a point at which something has happened, a thing to do: task, work, job, chore, errand, duty, etc.

Now read only a few of literally hundreds of quotations on time management; you'll see that is really is an ages-old problem.

Quotations on Time

Time is the nurse and breeder of all good.
—*Two Gentlemen of Verona*, Act V.

He that will not apply new remedies must expect new evils; for time is the greatest innovator.
—Francis Bacon.

Time will teach more than all our thoughts.
—Benjamin Disraeli.

He lives long that lives well, and time
misspent is not lived, but lost.
—Thomas Fuller

Time is money.
—Baron Lytton

To choose time is to save time.
—Francis Bacon.

There's a time for all things.
—*Comedy of Errors*, Act II

Our yesterdays follow us; they constitute and meaning to our
present deeds.
—Joseph Parker

Time is what we want most, but what alas! We use worst.
—William Penn.

Time is a merciless enemy, as it is also a merciless friend and
healer.
—Gandhi.

All that time is lost which might be better employed.
—Jean Jacques Rousseau.

SPACE

If we make space productive, will it reduce crime?
Would a result-minded-institution tolerate unused space?
Should we question the use of every square foot of space?
What would be ideal use of all available space?
How many more questions can we ask about space productivity?
All the above questions are answered with good management.

To maximize the use of space it is necessary to focus on each square foot of space. I have never seen a prison that does not have unused space which simple time management would improve. Think of it this way: if space is not used, it can be called "downtime," very much like any valuable piece of equipment which is not being used twenty-four hours per day. These unused areas can be used to increase the overall effectiveness of prisons. If inmates are responsible, as they should be, for their own learning they will find creative ways to use space. Only those inmates who are responsible, who want out, inmates motivated to return home, inmates who are tired of welfare, inmates who like productive work, inmates who like to be their own man, etc; will be able to discover maximum use of space. Prison managers get their pay, with or without results that make our streets a safe place to live. These managers incidentally are not "bad people," they just haven't realized how important their role is in their communities.

I often wonder, does anyone remember that Japan taught the world that the worker, on the line, who tightens the nuts and bolts is the person who can improve the quality of the work? Why do we assume that inmates do not have a brain that can improve the quality of prisons? What could be a more natural resource?

To magnify the value of space let's use the dictionary definition...

Definitions and Descriptions of Space

"Space is an area between or within things, an area or room for some purpose, extending without limits in all directions." In the business world every square foot of space needs to be productive. Every space has a cost factor. If it is not used in a productive way it increases the overall operation cost. Wasting space is considered poor management.

If a general statement can be made about anything, I think it can honestly be said that prisons make no valuable, productive use of space. They *do* confine people, but that is all that can be said for them. The question we should ask: why would any taxpayer tolerate the use of their money *to increase crime in their communities*? Because that is exactly what is happening.

Almost every person in prison will return to their community with few work or social skills, and without a philosophy that wants to improve his or her community. If an inmate is out to get all he can from his community, he is not giving back what he should. If space is maximized, and managed as it should be, inmates will find a quiet faith and confidence; their thinking will change. Every waking moment should be focused on their ability to improve the world they live in. There is a great need for leaders and many inmates can lead other inmates if they are encouraged to do so. This makes prison a better investment for society. "Is this the Pollyanna look?"

Absolutely. But, if they don't play (our game) they pay. They must manage their space or stay in the atmosphere; the jail they have created for themselves. Their "prison time" can be reduced, depending only on how hard they work at changing themselves and their peers.

MATERIAL

Most material found in a prison setting is used to confine the human body. No material is used to improve the human mind. To say, "What a fool I have been," is the only material of any value. I call it thinking, and it creates a change in attitude with an immediate need for personal growth. Focus on new ways of thinking will change who they have been, who they are today, and who they become.

To help inmates maximize their time in prison they need material to read, discuss, and write about. They need material that will change their thinking and help them learn how to learn. They need to learn that education begins today and should continue every day of their life. It's when they stop learning that they get themselves in trouble. Quotations can be found on: Attitude, growth, knowledge, love, marriage, parenting, self-respect, wisdom, and hundreds of other topics. Quotations are highly recommended by Winston Churchill, and many other successful people. They are useful for anyone with an open, learning mind. Let's look at some:

Quotations regarding the Material of Mind

The mind is a strange machine, which can combine the materials offered to it in the most astonishing ways, but without materials from the external world it is powerless.
—Bertrand Russell

An empty man is full of himself.
—Edward Abbey

The human mind is our fundamental resource.
—John Fitzgerald Kennedy.

A human being is not, in any proper sense, a human being till he is educated.
—Horace Mann.

Character development is the great, if not the sole, aim of education.
—William James O'Shea.

To make a statement that every problem has a solution may be considered by some to be unrealistic, or perhaps even foolish. Without optimism, however, we can be sure no problems will be solved. Without clear focus, while searching for results, we are ineffective.

Children cry, scream, and stamp with fury, unable to express their desires. As soon as they can speak and tell their want, and the reason of it, they become gentle."
—*Emerson.*

Perhaps our greatest need is to help students find a way to express their selves.

If the tongue had not been framed for articulation, man would still be a beast in the forest. The same weakness and want, on a higher plane, occurs daily in the education of ardent young men and women. Ah! you don't understand me; I have never met with any one who comprehends me: and they sigh and weep, write verses, and walk alone.
—*Emerson*

Teenagers in their volcanic condition become good citizens when they find someone who *listens* the way they think they should be listened to, and when they find someone who will discuss, what they think needs discussion.

Happy Students in Only One Hour a Day

Tight, focused, enthusiastic use of only one hour per day will improve the learning and success rate of students. It will help them "learn how to learn" in the way Carl R. Rogers suggested in his work. We should follow the teaching suggestions Carl Rogers has given us. Freedom in schools one hour each day will make a dramatic change in all schools.

My merchandising experience taught me, time management will boost results dramatically. I suggest if we used one hour in the same well managed way that a television show is programmed, perhaps this hour could be the most productive time of each school day. If we focus and maximize the use of time available, with the material students have an interest in, we can take education to a higher level without extra cost.

I have written earlier in this book about a basic exercise for this hour, namely giving students the time and materials to research the meaning and usage of a single word. In the previous chapters I have utilized this method to shed light directly on the points of education that need emphasis. Ask yourself now if that focus on words like Time, Space and Material, did not effectively promote lucid thought and consideration on the topic at hand…

Let me give an example of what happens to our thinking if we are focused on one word of interest. All activities we do from morning to bedtime, from brushing our teeth to a walk in the park, can give our subconscious mind an opportunity to focus. Whatever we are doing can remind us of what our focus is for the day. If our focus for the day is the word "courage" we will suffer from a disease Deer Hunters call "Buck Fever." Their imagination runs wild; they see a deer behind every bush, rock or tree.

The word courage will make an appearance in the same way, in some of the strangest places. *Courage* will be seen in TV commercials and dramas, in the lyrics of songs on the radio, in magazines, newspapers, conversations with friends, etc. As we work and play during the day, ideas for use of the word *courage* will come from many sources. If we intentionally do some research on courage our knowledge will deepen even more. We can become an expert on the word in a very short amount of school time comparatively, because we are actually *focusing* on it all day long.

Learning to make maximum use of one hour per day will help students make better use of every hour, all day. They will learn to focus, work on what they value most, and solve problems by breaking down hours into smaller segments that can be managed. They can become responsible for their own education. Almost everyone likes to be his or her own boss. Learning to be their own time management expert will help them become a stronger student in every class they attend.

27

The experiment, years ago, using Rogers' thinking was a failure because he did not realize freedom all day long was too much freedom. It became wasteful, it was nonproductive. Children need discipline; they can't grow without it. But, if we challenge them to learn on their own they will pull themselves up to learning far beyond expectations. I cannot imagine anyone rising to excellence, without the power to use some of their own thinking in some area of their life. We all become stronger if we take a risk on our own thinking. Even a mistake makes us stronger. Action right or wrong, with courage, takes us to a level far beyond where we thought possible.

Children grow and learn because that is their nature. Giving them freedom to grow at their own speed will magnify their learning dramatically. President Roosevelt suggested there is a need for the "joy of achievement and the thrill of creative effort," through learning.

Freedom will help eliminate the idea that schools exist to make everyone the same. We are not all the same. The most important work of the education system is to prove we are all special. No one else has the talent and ability we each individually have.

How Many People Do Not Have a College Degree?

We might ask the question: How many people do not have a college degree and how many are disappointed in themselves because of it?

The numbers are in the millions, and most of them will never have a college degree. It is in my opinion our national disgrace.

Yet, in spite of the lack of school contribution our citizens are successful. Is there any doubt that our schools are not giving the kind of service taxpayers have a right to expect? Many taxpayers have the foolish impression that their children are not college material. Many more don't like or are bored with the necessity of following the way ideas are presented in classrooms. This is easy to understand.

It is absolutely wrong for anyone to feel less than adequate because of a piece of paper, a college degree, that only a few have. Most people are capable, but they have decided not to go along with mass education thinking. We should be able to study what we want, not what self-appointed experts think is necessary. Learning, like work or life, should give us fulfillment. Most geniuses do not listen to experts or authority figures. They set their own goals, make their own plans, and work their plan.

I am sympathetic with those who are embarrassed because they have no college degree. These people have been totally ignored by the education system. They have fallen between the cracks of our society, but they are not to be felt sorry for. Many have found and used the street-way of thinking for themselves. Freedom from an academic point of view can be a useful source of learning. Success is often just finding a need and filling it.

Many stories have been told about men and women who. have failed to strive for things they want in life. Because of the education system, they feel inadequate and unworthy. They feel they are less than the man, or woman, they could be. If the truth were known, they are often better citizens and parents than most. *Over seventy percent of our population has no college degree.* Wouldn't this be a terrible country to live in if a college degree was the only way to become a decent citizen? The world has more than its share of educated derelicts!

For years women have taken the back seat in education. They often see themselves as just a housewife or just a secretary. The fear they develop often overwhelms them. Their success or fulfillment in life is less because of it. There is no reason for anyone not to fulfill himself or herself in every way possible. We all have more potential than we realize and *the use of our talent does not require college*.

Achievement is not based on someone else's measurement. Keeping up with the Jones family next door has nothing to do with finding and using the good things about our self.

Education is Not Necessarily a Reflection of "IQ"

People are not necessarily successful because they have a college degree. They are a success because they are natural learners, who follow their own instinct, their own curiosity. They are people who ask questions and intentionally look for answers. They are people who could have learned without organized classes.

The above statement can be true or false depending on the student. Every successful person is an individual and every success is individual.

There are often statistics published that try to prove college students make more money during their lifetime. This may be true but I believe this will change as people learn to educate themselves. Computers are going to make this possible, and in fact the stories of "under-educated" nerds who made it big in the boom of computer games, software, and the expansion of the Internet are now commonplace.

In some cases, it is not a person's lack of qualifications that hold them back; it's a lack of a degree. This is a judgment placed on individuals by a society that doesn't care to take the time to hire the best people, but the best resumes. These same people may have found success, if there had been no such thing as a college degree.

Of course, there are also exceptions to this rule. Young people in college meet lifetime friends. Those friends help each other through life. They develop the habit of being successful just by being around each other. They often use the network system as a source of survival; they promote each other.

The good-old-boys system works well in both small and large companies. Friends undoubtedly promote friends; in fact, this is a significant contributor to mediocrity in many companies. We are just now beginning to break this habit of promoting people who are not as productive as they should be.

Part of the reason our business world has failed to keep up with competition is because we allow a college degree more value than it is worth. Too many degrees have been given that only prove the student was persistent. Degrees are also given because the student has agreed to suffer through or tolerate the mediocrity of the system. This does not prove the student is the appropriate hire for the workplace. It has been suggested in some circles that this rewarding of drudge-like persistence is just creating a slightly more decorated level of assembly-line worker. On the other hand, that persistence may come from patience and intelligence. It may prove a good quality, if the graduate also has the courage to adapt to non-academic pressures, evolve, and hustle, when it seems appropriate.

Learning is a habit, and a good place to develop a habit is to associate with people who are also learning. There are problems, however, with this atmosphere. In mass education everyone is learning the same thing, so successful students must breakaway from the mold of sameness. Successful people don't follow the same path everyone else has a tendency to use. How do they do this?

Students Need the Freedom to Be Who They Are… and Become Who They Will Be

"So much does the soul require an object at which to aim," wrote Montaigne, "that when it does not have one, it will turn its violence upon itself, and create a false and fantastic problem, in which it does not even believe, rather than not have something to work upon."

Through my many years with the California Youth Authority people have often asked me: "Why is there so much juvenile delinquency? If I could give only one answer, Montaigne's above quotation would be my reply. Parents and teachers foolishly think they can slow or stop the explosion of a stick of dynamite. All children need is a good coach who will lead them in the direction

31

they truly want to go. A good coach is listening and ready for the next unknown challenge.

My one word goals, that are actually the first steps in the search for wisdom, will help them burn the candle at both ends if necessary, and utilize their energies so they will not have to say "I'm bored," which is a common problem with children addicted to television.

Most of the quotations from great thinkers in history seem to agree that education is something we do for ourselves. Mass education seems to run counter to this, and in fact, some very famous thinkers have voiced the opinion that it is actually destructive. Do we need to take such sides that seem to make a solution to educational concerns impossible? I suggest that there has to be a middle ground.

History points out that most progress, inventions, or creativity of any kind are the result of previous experiments. All creativity and learning rides on the shoulders of someone before them. Carl R. Rogers believed it necessary that teachers allow students the right to use their own enthusiasm to drive the speed of their learning. He liked the idea of self-education.

I want to combine the use of his thinking along with the apparent necessity of mass education. All that's necessary is that we allow students to follow their curiosity and enthusiasm. Students need a good balance of both freedom and focus to magnify and speed their learning.

The best thing about this is that whether you are a parent or a teacher, you can implement the hour a day plan without having to worry about "changing the system" or "revolutionizing education." To spell it out even more clearly— you can do it without waiting for foot-dragging administrators to "adopt" it as a "strategy for education." Skip the board meetings and go right to the source; buy some reference books and give them to your kids or your students.

Learning how to learn is the result of students digging for their own information on each subject. As I have mentioned before, the subject should be one simple word to reduce confusion. The teacher's purpose is to facilitate learning—not to teach. There should be no grades, evaluation, or judgment of any kind during a one-hour period. Students can write their own book at any time of the day or night.

They will be learning about the problems and successes of people, not dates and places that have nothing to do with successful living. The focus will be on how people feel, think, and how they have solved the problems of daily living. I have been asked so many times; "How is knowing the date 1492 going to put money in my wallet so I can feed my kids?"

Kids, like a good business executive, want to know what the bottom line is. If they must waste time they want to do it in their own way. They have little patience with a teacher who is just filling in time. This is an ideal time for them to focus on a self-designed project of their own. Learning about their favorite word is a great use of their energy while thinking about how they are going to be famous or simply daydreaming.

Students will develop what could be called a liberal education if they have the opportunity. They will develop a quiet faith and confidence because of the effort they initiated on their own. They will learn how to solve their own problems. They will become individuals, not a member of "the gang."

The first thing a child should learn is how to endure. It is what he will have most need to know.
—Jean-Jacques Rousseau

Individualism Is the Answer, Not College

Incidentally, I am not against college, if that is what you want to do. I have already discussed the negative social effect of not having a college degree when looking for gainful employment. I am saying, however, you will get more out of college if you apply some of the information found in this book.

Ask anyone who can be called successful by our standards; most would agree, college is only a training ground. It's an atmosphere where learning is taking place and the habit of success is being formed. No one gets any stronger, physically or mentally with out testing their own strength. It's wrong to think, however, that the only place you can learn and the only place you can test yourself is in college. High School is also a training ground, which could be an effective beginning for lifelong learning.

An important advantage of college is the fact that it is an opportunity to focus on a specific subject. Successful people learn to focus; but it is a habit that can be developed anywhere, anytime. Comments from Sir Winston Churchill help prove my point: "I have no technical and no university education, and have just had to pick up a few things as I went along."

Our Schools Don't Reflect Our Society

Our schools and homes need to include practical books and information. We have focused too much on the basics and teaching methods. The following quotation can have a dramatic effect on the education of our children:

I agree with Plutarch, that Aristotle did not waste his great pupil's time on lessons in the construction of syllogisms, or on the principles of geometry, but taught him wise precepts on the subject of valor, prowess, magnanimity, temperance, and that assurance, which knows no fear.
—Montaigne

In other words he did not teach rules of logic and deduction, or the principles of geometry, but taught him wise rules on the subject of courage, physical skills, and to have self-respect for the individual he is. He taught him to think on a grand scale, with strength and power of his own design. He taught him that he could make a difference in the world. Personal self-restraint was important to him. He taught him ambition, generosity, forgiveness, liberalism and tolerance. He taught him to be comfortable with himself. Self-respect was important with self-assurance that knows no fear.

The ultimate goal of the education system is to shift to the individual the burden of pursuing his own education.
—John W. Gardner

Note: if you want some new/old thinking on education, refer to the education quotations in the second part of this book.

The inspirational and motivational needs of our young people are critically important. They need to see themselves as at least, an amateur intellectual, a thinker with possibilities. There is a creative need in all of us that ignites enthusiasm for new thoughts and ideas. A lifetime of creativity helps us be useful, responsible and effective people. Creativity helps us find and use our natural talent and ability.

The responsibility of parents and teachers is not to teach facts, figures and symbols. The responsibility is to develop a love, and excitement for learning. If learning could be measured for a lifetime, I believe it would rank as the highest and most exciting lifetime activity.

Parents, if they want successful children, must aggressively take their children to new adventures that stretch their minds. Stretch them so they will no longer think the same thoughts over and over. We all have the same strange habit of thinking the same thoughts endlessly, forever and forever. This habit reduces the learning curve dramatically. Students must move on to something new. The one hour of independent, creative, self-motivated learning accomplishes this. The action created and the fun of moving in the direction of new thinking, new ideas, and perhaps even wisdom can easily replace the energy used by adults to control children. Adults today are obsessed with control; sometimes just because of habit, fear, or because they are not happy with their own academic achievement. Often they are controllers because their parents controlled them. The shortage of freedom to become an individual is a cycle that must be broken.

Parents and teachers who have a quiet faith and confidence in themselves seldom find the need or have the desire to control anyone. Controllers are people with fear in their veins. Children can get excited about well-placed discipline, but control is the most destructive word in the English language. If we have a management problem with youth, it is partly because we suffer from over-use of control.

All teenagers are hungry for the adventure of being oneself, not a copy of their parents; but to become a person of their own design.

CHAPTER 4

Leadership (pt 1)

A Ph.D. is a Scholar, Not a Leader

We can I think safely say, that all of our education leaders have a Ph.D. I have come to the conclusion that a person who speaks through the credibility of a Ph.D. may not be practical or able to lead us to education excellence. Truthfully, the rough and tumble lessons we learn in life do not come from books.

I don't like to be the bad guy; but think about this. Almost every community in America has a person with a Ph.D. who is in charge of our School District. How many is that? A million? I don't know, but I do know they follow each other like sheep running over a mountain cliff. Perhaps one-half dozen stand out, and they spend most of their time helping the business world make millions of dollars. Those in Education, those who have an immediate effect on our children, have been ignored. What is wrong here?

This idea just occured to me: Why do we choose people as leaders who do not live in the real world, the one we live in everyday of our life? Do yourself and your community a favor. Look up the word "academic" in your dictionary. Two of mine give this description: Theoretical; not practical, relative or directly useful.

Learned or scholarly but lacking in worldliness, common sense, or practicality. Conforming to set rules, standards, or traditions; conventional. Too far from immediate reality; not practical enough; too speculative…wow! How does that hit you?

Another question: how many of you go to an academic when you have other practical needs, like a toothache or a broken bone, or the flu? or a flat tire? or a leaky roof?

Now do some research on this word: *leadership*. To make it easy, read my collection of quotations in Chapter Eleven. Is it not true that lack of leadership is clearly—and without question—the reason for school failure? In fact, would there be less crime in America if our schools had the attention of our children? Of course it is not the only reason; but how can we scientifically measure the truth. How do we know unless we test the quality of leadership?

Perhaps a test of excellence is really how our children behave when they are alone. These questions we should ask ourselves: If schools were not mandatory would students attend because they want to? Is there any indication in our communities that schools are being lead by a strong leader? Is our leader out on the floor where the problems are, or is he hiding behind the big mahogany desk enjoying his own little comfort zone? Most important of all, are students, teachers, principals, and parents happy to see their leader, and is he or she glad to see them? Is it obvious he or she is struggling with us; feeling our pain? Is our leader teaching how to maximize time, space, and material? I remember, when I was very young, my supervisor threatened to nail my office door shut. Perhaps? No, that wouldn't be nice.

The life of a Ph.D. has been sheltered between the pages of books; they have never been fired from a job because of lack of performance. They have not had to meet a weekly payroll or suffered from their own inability to sell or manufacture a product. They focus on ideas but if they are wrong or ineffective their discipline may be only a letter in their employee file, or perhaps a lack of consideration for the next promotion. Being effective has not been a life or death consideration. Their experience in my opinion is incomplete. God knows we need them, and they are certainly an important part of our academic world; but I don't think anyone would deny their leadership has and is the reason our young people think of themselves as second-class citizens today. They have been our leaders, they are responsible, but they have clearly failed to solve our education problems.

I would never recommend "radical changes," but I do suggest that we help students grasp and work with the concept that teachers can facilitate the students learning, and help students make use of their own curiosity and enthusiasm. We should not buy them fish; we should buy them a fishing pole. The effectiveness of our schools will improve when we find the courage to give students creative freedom. They need encouragement that will allow them to work with and solve as many of their own problems as possible.

It is a well-known fact, in the field of individual counseling, that most people have a solution to their own problem, all they need is a "sounding board." They need someone who will listen to them so they can discover what they think about their problem.

People of all ages like to design solutions of their own.

This coincides well with Emerson's thinking that young people need respect. Most people, young or old, will rise to the occasion when they have been promoted to a position or status that appears to be respectable. Young people are real people, who just happen to have short legs. They have qualities you and I will never have; so they deserve respect, as much as any responsible adult.

If you can live the following quotation, you will find that you have more courage to impart the freedom to young people than you may have realized.

If I distrust the human being then I must cram him with information of my own choosing, lest he go his own mistaken way. But if I trust the capacity of the human individual for developing his own potentiality, then I can provide him with many opportunities and permit him to choose his own way and his own direction in his learning.
—Carl R. Rogers

'You Now Have a Quiet Faith and Confidence in Yourself.'

If you read this quotation often enough, it will become a part of your philosophy. If you associate with young people, your thinking will rise above your present level of awareness and patience. If you think about this "deeply," with an open mind and heart, you will discover the defects of your own parent and teacher relationships.

A Good Coach Has a Better Team Each Year

A school principle that wants motivated teachers helps them grow each year into more effective teachers. The best leaders ask questions, and help their associates find answers to their problems.

The only way to focus on growth is to eliminate unnecessary busy work. Leadership in schools has not yet discovered personal growth, the kind that improves their work. Consequently schools are not improving each year, as they should be. The biggest challenge and purpose for a manager is to improve results year after year. If schools are not improving each year they are falling behind, which is exactly what the records show. Whether you judge schools by declining test scores, rising numbers of "social promotions," or any other criteria, they seem to be treading water and running out of breath.

Confusion, frustration and fear, are the only alternative some parents and teachers think they have. That alternative brings means of trying to control students, instead of trying to educate them by helping them learn to learn for themselves. This is sad and they are wrong. As it happens, today parents think there is a need for even more control. This is destroying our schools. This attitude will destroy the small amount of self-respect students have. Working in this prison-like environment will eventually destroy the morale of teachers, and will certainly disappoint our children.

Managers who have a quiet faith and confidence never feel the need or have the desire to control anyone. A strong leader knows that the thinking of employees and clients is the source of all progress. Learning is a natural process that flows like a river finding its own way. Teachers must make use of any natural interest or ability students have. They must play to the student's strengths, not to their weaknesses.

A manager, as suggested by Dr. Peter Drucker, must maximize the teachers ability to use time, place, and material so the job can be efficiently done. School teachers and managers should share the responsibility and credit for success. A leader should not be a leader unless they can make a difference. If the word "leadership" does not mean constant interest and a constant study, leaders will destroy more success than they build.

I repeat a valuable quotation: *Not all readers are leaders, but all leaders are readers.* A good coach has the courage to pick players who add to the strength of the team. Incidentally, the one quality all leaders have, and they should do it everyday, is the ability to teach... They should teach us how to solve problems before and after they appear.

Let us look at an important question that follows naturally from the discussion above: *How does a good teacher teach?*

There are many ways: grammar is used as a negative tool to correct mistakes rather than being used in a positive way to encourage hard work. Use of a positive approach can inspire the feeling: "I'm winning, improving, and getting better everyday." If the focus on grammar is destroying our students it is destroying our schools and our society. The use of correct grammar in writing should be learned like hitting a baseball is learned: by voluminous swinging— at words. Too much correction will deaden the spiritual confident swing. Of all the mistakes teachers make, this is the biggest of all. It immediately stops focus. It even deadens enthusiasm. It creates doubt about what the goal should be. Doubt is the death of interest in personal growth. This is where we start to hear the words, "What's the use?"

A Sense of History

If students see their history, their level of past learning, it will show where they used to be. A view of old work makes them smile. It will add hope, which makes them not ashamed. It makes them want to play the game and set the goals they could help establish. Hope is a dynamic force that inspires goals many have never dreamed possible.

Work: The Foundation of Happiness

The grand essentials to happiness in this life are: Something to do, Something to love, Something to hope for.
—*Joseph Addison*

Optimism is the source of every success. If we raise the level of optimism in schools, students will try harder and succeed more often.

Is there a way to turn pessimism into action? I don't think so. I am often amazed at the lack of optimism seen in the world today. It seems the nature of "man" is to find something wrong with everything. I don't understand this kind of thinking. My experience as a young man was with the J.J. Newberry Company, the fastest growing retail chain in the 1950s. This experience, as a merchandiser, taught me to believe there was a solution for every problem. Solving problems can be exhilarating. It becomes a habit and a positive way of living. It takes us closer to our goals.

Mr. Newberry was an eternal optimist. He wrote his managers a letter every week trying to spread the good word. I remember a theme that ran through many of his letters. He believed, that if I was a manager, there was an obligation to be a leader in my community. In one letter he suggested we ask our fellow merchants this question, "How is business?" He said, the answer each time would be, "Business is lousy." We tried it. He was right. Comments were often to the effect that the "weather is bad," "it's too hot," "its raining again," "the wholesale costs are too high," "look at this junk, it's made out of Japanese beer cans!"…you get the picture. This was in the 1950s, when Japan was searching for new ways to create business. Look at the results today. Was Japan optimistic? Is the Pope Catholic?

In my experience, with the California Youth Authority, the same mentality prevailed. Many of the Youth Counselors I worked with had very little faith in young people and even less in the parents. And the parents, who often visited on weekends, saw nothing but gloom and doom. We called them Champions of the Bad News Bears. In our daily life we often listen to complaining about unemployment, high taxes, and politicians who are less than honest. It's true we have some problems, but we are living better than most people on this earth. We need to face the issues head on, and one of the questions is:

"How Can We Solve Our Problems if We Don't *Think* We Can?"

We are in a desperate need; and that need is for optimism. If we believe every problem has a solution there must be a way out of this destructive cycle. "Why mop the floor if we don't expect a shine?" "Why wash the windows if we don't expect a work of art?" "Why care, listen, love, think, teach, and get married without expecting things will be better than they are?" Why *not* optimism?

We have a word for this in our language. This word leads to optimism. It is attitude. An optimistic attitude creates personal growth. It helps us see possibilities. It creates courage, vision and action. Attitude can be good or bad and it leads to success or failure. The choice we make is our own.

It's important that we feel a quiet faith and confidence with ourselves. We need to think we are intellectually moving ahead in a way that feels like personal growth. Our thinking helps make it so.

As a Man Thinketh by James Allen proves my point. It is one of the great books of all time. Everyone should have the privilege of reading it. This book should be required reading for every high school student in America.

My mission, my passion, is to consolidate thinking that school administrators have missed. Their decisions are being made with incomplete information. I am amazed that no one seems to understand the problems and solutions. We clearly have not listened to the great thinkers! Many had opinions on education that have been ignored. My passion wakes me up in the middle of the night. I have no doubt in my mind that I know what teenagers want and need. Writing helps me, and it will help students learn something new each day. It makes us more interesting to ourselves and to others. Plain and simple, it just makes life for everyone more fun....

I like to see the wisdom of the old, in young people, and the young of age, in old people.
—Emerson.

I write what comes off the top of my head, without worrying about what others may think. Since no teacher needs to read their homework, this is a great opportunity for students to be open and honest, to be exactly who they are. There is no need for them to pretend or to be something experts think they should be. I'm often surprised with the words that fall from my pen. I'm motivated to work as the amateur that I am; while learning from experience and daily practice. As the Nike shoe ads say: "Just Do It."

I think it is obvious this is what I have done. Writing is that simple. I hope students will join me in this adventure. Words that work, words that seem to sound right, help us learn on our own. So many times we don't know what we think until we have written it down. It's a hands-on crafty kind of thing that makes sense. It solidifies the thoughts we think.

I am like a child with a new hammer that thinks everything needs to be hammered. We are all by nature, creative and we can't help ourselves. Being creative is what we should do at every opportunity. I believe young people should create something everyday. A short period of time should be scheduled into their life for creativity. Not because someone has asked them, but because they want to. They should write a mini-essay or poem everyday. It should be private and no one has to correct it. Taxpayers do not need to pay a teacher to read it.

Our leaders, those who pull the strings, are totally confused about the needs of our students. Although it's not true in all cases, it appears many want to make the problem complex to justify their job. Many administrators are too busy being mature, wise, or all knowing. "Machoism" often interferes with the clarity of their thinking. Their listening skills need improvement.

There is a way to continue growing and changing every day of our life. It's so simple it's hard to believe it has not been done before. It works so easily, so naturally, it seems to follow your own inclination. It's not drudgery, but fun and interesting, so it becomes learning without effort all day, every day. This learning process is a way to catalogue what we enjoy and want to learn.

Because of continuing growth our interests are many. We can use one word for each interest. These words are like a hook on the inside of our closet. Our subconscious mind becomes a warehouse of ideas. When we use these words they act as a guide to help us collect information on everything we see, hear, or read.

My own motivation for doing what I do is, first of all, that I enjoy learning. Secondly, I believe we could all be more than we claim to be. A carpenter, if he is good at what he does, must learn to be more than a carpenter. A gardener must be more than a gardener. A doctor must be more than the professional they claim to be. A parent must be more than a parent; a wife or husband must be more than just partners. To think we are "more" opens up a new world of hope and maybe boldness.

Truly, knowledge or expertise in a specialty sinks deeper because of focus. A liberal education of our own design broadens our interests. It gives us a quiet faith and confidence, which no one can explain. It's a "warm fuzzy feeling" that makes us different from all of our friends and family.

We are all individuals; we need to listen to ourselves, respect and celebrate our individuality.

RESPECT for ourselves proves we are honestly listening.
LISTENING helps us put action to work with our own thinking.
CELEBRATION is having the courage to take a risk on our thinking.

Being an amateur of many things is the best way I know to personally grow in ways we enjoy. When we admit we are amateurs and enjoy working as an amateur we are taking a risk on ourselves without the fear of making mistakes. It's a learning process that changes who we are. Our hobby could be the gathering of information we enjoy thinking about. *A good way to learn is with research and writing things we wish we knew more about.* If we make it a habit of writing what we hear and think, it helps us discover our real truth. The liberal education we can give ourselves makes us an amateur of many things and an expert where we want to focus.

Here is what works for me. I use my one hundred words as hooks for my learning. These words, which could be for all of us, become our own word selection. They can help us guide our learning. They define who we are and want to be. The fun, and the adventure of life is in the game. To clarify, simplify, and discipline our selves we can focus on just one word. But, to increase our volume of writing we sometimes just write to see what happens next. In other words, we write as fast as we can about what ever we think. Our fingers get tired, but we continue anyway. Our intention is to get as many words on paper as we can in a specific period of time. Only a small percent of this "free-flowing" kind of writing has any value, but the habit and the results could be a surprise.

Many years ago I learned that if I have a job to do, it would be necessary to break it down into its smallest possible exercise or activity. We can do anything we make up our minds to do if we focus on and understand the smallest part.

We can build a brick house if we focus on one brick at a time. If we explore the value of each brick or word of interest, we will find that our house or our learning is truly of our own design. I believe that anyone can learn and teach whatever their interest or enthusiasm leads them to.

One Word One Hour a Day Works for Any Age

Since many of us are members of the "over the hill" age group, we're also concerned with fulfillment and self-expression of life. Loneliness, or a lack of satisfaction with our life, is so unnecessary. Most will agree that "we are what we think about." Self-education can truly lead us to the fountain of youth and usefulness. I believe our thinking habits make us what we are.

Orel Hershiser believes our attitude is crucial. He said, "Success begins and ends, and the pitcher succeeds or fails, with the all-important next pitch." He believes in excellence and devotion to the task. His attitude expresses commitment and responsibility for the total use of his talent. He believes his work is to make maximum use of all the tools God has given him.

I am one who believes we die on the inside when we stop changing and growing. We need to be actively involved, improving how we think and act everyday of our life. Life's fulfillment depends on using all of the ability and talent we have. Our potential is endless. It increases, expands, or multiplies itself as we use it. Like the human body, muscles anywhere will help other muscles strengthen themselves. They each affect and support each other. Weak thoughts or muscles grow stronger because of their relationship with strong thoughts and muscles.

This work is not complete and never will be. It's my hope that we will complete it in our own individual way. If we get tough with our self and follow our own thinking it will take us where we want to go. It's also my hope that it will lead us to constant change and the realization that the wisdom you find will be our own. We have earned it. The search will change us. It will change the effect we have on both our family and friends.

Jean Piaget said, "Every time we teach a child something we keep him from inventing it himself."

I would go a step further. Every time we teach a child something, rather than helping him learn, we keep him from inventing himself.

"By its very nature, teaching homogenizes both its subject and its objects. Learning, on the other hand, liberates. The more we know about ourselves and the world, the freer we are to achieve everything we are capable of achieving."

—Warren Bennis
On Becoming a Leader, p. 70

Our Institutions Have Let Us Down

Most of us who have worked in private industry have noticed there is a constant effort to improve business results over the previous year. Personal growth is a lifestyle, and absolutely necessary. A seminar can be found for every working skill.

This growth mentality, however, is not necessarily found in Education and other Civil Service employment. Most schools and prisons in America are over-managed because Civil Service managers don't understand productivity. The lack of courage and the fear managers have of "making mistakes" prevents their understanding of the growth process. Rather than seeing themselves as a normal (i.e., vulnerable) human being who is learning from mistakes, their mistakes stifle and control their life. Incidents control policy, instead of policy controlling incidents.

Decisions are not made on the job; they are made at the State Capitol. Macho managers who have a chance to make a difference seldom have the courage to make a mistake. They are unnecessarily prideful; if they had to create a profit like most of us, they would lose their "shirts."

Successful managers don't worry about mistakes, they worry that they are not giving the kind of service their clients need.

Most teachers know that mistakes are the source of all learning. Mistakes are the driving force that creates excellence simply because everyone wants to get it right. School administrators have to know this. If mistakes are a driving force for the students, open-minded school managers are capable of learning the same way.

Mistakes should help invent courageous new programs; instead they create additional paperwork, new manuals with new rules, regulation, and paranoia. Paper work replaces managers who make on the spot decisions.

The drowsiness of institutions replaces all signs of living, breathing people. Established policy is the death of improvement and change which should be never ending. Our managers can be compared to the captain of a ship at sea. If they ignore the wind and the rain their shipment will arrive where it is not needed. Employees are not allowed to think, act, and fill a need that is obvious to the naked eye. The cost is phenomenal.

Where Are Our Leaders?

Because we are a democracy there will never be a time when all of our problems are solved.

Because the nature of democracy demands change, leadership must think and act as needed.

Because we are people not robots, there will always be new problems we have not faced.

Because the manual for life is different for each of us, decisions must be made as problems occur.

Because science has come to few conclusions we must go where new knowledge takes us.

Because decision-making manuals are out of date by the time they're printed, strong leadership is necessary.

When we send a ship to the moon it is off course 90% of the time. Because of this problem, leadership must change its direction constantly. No decision is, or ever will be, final.

I have found when I put my toe in the river my toe has changed and so has the river.
—Unknown, based on Heraclitus

If we can agree that change is a constant, we must also deal with costs. I hope you don't mind if I take this opportunity to express a "taxing" opinion: our tax dollar use is scandalous. Students, by their very nature, love to learn, so tell me why should anything so wonderful and natural be expensive? The great truth is, when you shovel sand against the tide, it will be expensive.

Over-management by managers who have fear in their veins creates unnecessary expense. Mostly for the benefit of the student, but also in the interest of dollar tax value, we need to learn the nature of children. The more control we expect, the less we have. Human beings are not controllable, but they can be motivated with freedom. If teachers do less teaching and facilitate more learning our costs will fall dramatically.

What an opportunity! Children need a short period of time each day to run, as hard and fast as they can. They can imitate a young colt in a green pasture: with the new, the fresh, the excitement, of early morning.

They need to make their own path in a twenty-acre pasture of creative freedom. A few minutes each day of self-designed learning can become education at its best. All of this can be done in the interest of finding how good they are at something; anything, they dont care what.

A Balance of Freedom and Discipline

Students follow their curiosity, enthusiasm, and natural ability. Children need more goals and fewer rules.

If our schools are actively creative, well managed, they can help children be responsible for their own confidence, courage, and honesty. "Not held responsible," but learning to be responsible in the short period of only one hour per day. Solid citizens are happier when they know they are carrying part of the load.

Children have integrity too. All people of all ages are happier when they have a responsibility, "a work" of some kind that contributes to the overall cause. More and more in the workplace today, adult employees want to help managers accomplish their goals. They want to be a part of the solution. Modern managers of today are making it possible for employees to help maximize the use of time, space, and material.

Tis education forms the common mind,
Just as the twig is bent, the tree's inclined.
—Alexander Pope

Confidence, Courage, Honesty

I repeat this quotation because it is so important.

"So much does the soul require an object at which to aim," wrote Montaigne, "that when it does not have one, it will turn its violence upon itself, and create a false and fantastic problem, in which it does not even believe, rather than not have something to work upon."

With students, the energy is there, it won't go away, so this energy must learn the academic meaning of confidence, courage, listening, love, etc. These are words they have an interest in. Incidentally I would rather have a high-spirited child who knows what he wants than to have one who is afraid of his own shadow. I think of a happy child as a high-spirited racehorse who stays on the track and loves every minute of it. A parent's job is to be just-a-little-bit "more" high spirited than their child, with the patience to discipline and train; all this, based on love. All children need is a good teacher/coach who is tough enough to follow where students want to go, and still, stay-one-step ahead of them.

It's a competitive race in which the parent has to always be the winner, without the child feeling totally controlled. (If you are the big man with the big stick you will always be just the big man with the big stick.) Parenting is not for sissies or for someone who is not sure of who they are, where they want to go, and what is important in their life.

An appropriate quotation about Willie Shoemaker, perhaps the greatest of all Jockeys: "The horse never knew he was there, until the horse needed him."

How happy our children would be if they thought they were running their own race; searching for personal knowledge...at this moment.

They can be an intellectual amateur of their own design. They will, if we have the courage to allow them, show us what they can do. A good coach knows how to do this. We so often forget; every person on this earth has a different toolbox to work with.

This fact by itself should cause us to look at students in wonder. Will the next generation of children be the ones who help us find peace on this earth? What kind of problems can they solve we haven't? A good coach is listening and ready for the next unknown; in fact, they look forward to the next challenge. They teach confidence, courage, and they insist on honesty. Have you ever tried to manipulate a coach so you can play ball on his or her team? No, this is where the rubber meets the road, a sincere effort, an honest performance cannot be faked.

My one-word goals that search for wisdom will help them burn the candle at both ends if that's what it takes to keep them out of trouble. They will not have to say; "I'm bored," which is a common problem with children when the television is turned off.

Let them wrestle with their own choice of words, one at a time. Let them find their own wisdom.

I want to promote freedom of expression for children who have not yet been stifled by the dullness of classrooms. I'd like to promote true, honest amateurism, so children can be mini-experts on the many things that interest them. I'd like to promote a self-designed liberal education that follows what people enjoy doing with their life.

It was Thoreau who wrote in *Walden*, "Most people live their entire life in a quiet desperation."

The intensity of a goal should compare with the "final kick" needed while running to the end of a long race. We are all capable of more than we realize. Since we are all different, we should celebrate our individualism and search for that special talent not yet discovered.

The many questions I have asked school dropouts clearly indicates the fear of "sounding-like-a-fool," is the reason for most failure in school. To my amazement, like almost everything in life, simplicity is the best answer. With careful listening my conclusion is: both parents and teachers intimidate children with what they believe is correct English.

The best way to teach children what to think is with example. Let them see how you live, who you are, and who you would like to be. Teach them to set both short and long term goals with time limits. Write them down on paper; children like that habit.

The only rules children must follow should be physical things like: Brush your teeth, wash your hands, clean your room, wash the dishes, put out the trash, etc. If you tell them what to think, you short-circuit their thinking ability. Instead of this you can facilitate learning by making it obvious with your actions what you believe.

The reality is, after they learn to think for them-selves they may accept what you believe or they may-not. But, we cannot control them forever. There are times when all we can do is pray a lot. Another cold reality, if you insist they think like you, you

53

could have a teenage revolt on your hands. They will, like it or not, think for themselves and eventually become their own person. Don't ruin a lifetime party by insisting they imitate you.

Faith in Our Students is Our Best Control

Having their respect is permission to give them guidance.

Let me repeat a quotation from Rogers: "Adults who think that children must be manipulated for their own good have developed the attitude of a controlling parent who lacks faith in himself, the child, or humanity."

If I were training racehorses, I would discipline them enough to keep them on the track. But, too much discipline would cause them to forget how much fun the race is. Our children need directed freedom, not control that stifles learning, imagination, and creativity.

Teenagers Need Practical Information

If there is a "Dunce" in any class room that needs to be disciplined for lack of performance their punishment should be to write the above words on the blackboard one thousand times. To become human, to have good manners and respect for others is the basic reason for attending school.

For some reason self respect (consequently a clear conscience,) and social skills have taken the back seat in our classrooms. Isn't about time we asked why?

We must never forget that children are basically good. If we do not keep that in our mind at all times we are all in deep trouble.

They will prove our assumption is correct. They have no fear if you back them into a corner, and I don't blame them one-bit. I can't think of a reason to back anyone into a corner where they have no way out. No dignity left!

Outstanding Books on Leadership

There are many books that will keep our children in a high spirited frame of mind. Teachers can pick and choose useful ideas for classes.

A good example is a book that has sold more copies than any book, world wide, except for the Bible. For forty years that I know of this book has been totally ignored by high school and college teachers. Yet, I would bet my next month paycheck that most teachers and parents have read it. They have read it because they want to be effective as a person, they believe in good manners and respect for their fellow man, and they realize there is such a thing as diplomacy and good public relations. They practice listening because they want to be listened to.

This book teaches, the best conversationalist is always the best listener. Readers of this book believe there is a solution to every human relations problem. The fact that they believe it takes them closer to good communications. This is the way they live their life.

This book is *How To Win Friends and Influence People* by Dale Carnegie. It's strange that teachers have not been willing to share, at least, some of these ideas with their students. Apparently the title makes it the kind of book that is bought only when no one else is looking. If teachers want to influence other people they want no one to know about their intentions. How foolish. Carnegie had no sly intentions, he simply was trying to tell us where and how to find self-respect with practical social skills..

Criticism after writing the book caused him to make this comment: "My research came from Chesterfield and Jesus; if you don't listen to them, whom would you listen to?"

Our children need a clear conscience. Self-respect is the only way they will find it. To not know how to find self-respect is the tragedy of our time.

Dale Carnegie has it: love, peace, and respect for all. We must not forget all adults are "teachers." Our first responsibility is to teach living with friends and family.

At the risk of becoming simplistic, or perhaps even foolish, I must say, I truly believe if some of the ideas in this book were made required reading for High School Students, their social skills would rise dramatically.

Learning would become more important, gangs would become a thing of the past, drugs less important, and crime would return to normal. Like the old days, in many communities, locking the front door would seldom be necessary. Walking the streets at night would be a renewed pleasure.

Another outstanding book, *The Seven Habits of Highly Effective People* by Stephen R. Covey is a book of real value to young people. It is not a book that students will find easy to read, but many of these ideas should be part of thinking that leads to happiness.

Mentally Tough by Dr. James E. Loehr and Peter J. McLaughlin has useful information on success through focus and discipline.

A Road Less Traveled by M. Scott Peck M.D. is so valuable everyone who wants to think and act for him- or herself should read it. We should all copy quotations that fit our thinking and lifestyle. If students take this book seriously they could easily design their own education.

Another book is *Live Your Dreams* by Les Brown. Every senior in High School should read this book, or at least be made aware of the writer and his ideas. He is presently making history, which cannot be ignored.

Unlimited Power by Anthony Robbins has been a national best seller. His book is about setting goals and he shows how to reach them. Private industry is very excited about these books I have mentioned. There are many more, perhaps even better, that discuss respect for ideas that are not their own, negotiations, productivity, and how to manage their time. All of these books are written to encourage personal growth.

56

I continue asking myself this question: Why do schools ignore such practical thinking?

Information that has created success in the business world can improve our schools. It seems to me our professors, our leaders in education; need to come down out of the clouds. They need to lead us to simple, practical ideas that are obvious to successful people. Life is not as complicated as academia, our college professors, would like us to think.

The truth is, our problems are not simple, but there is hope. The need for self respect is at an all time high. The desire for learning comes natural with our youth. Our education leaders need to listen carefully to their clients.

The problems in our schools are management and leadership more than a teacher problem. And too often administrators, without realizing it, allow teachers to get in the way of their own goals. We must ask ourselves this question: Is there a situation, anytime, anywhere that became a success without good management and leadership? These two words, outside of prayer, are probably the most powerful words in the English language.

Good managers in every successful industry know the value of keeping employees focused on what is important, yet our teachers fail to discuss or analyze practical ideas. I believe Aristotle while teaching Alexander The Great would have used parts of these books.

I'm convinced growth is possible every day of our life. Most of you who work in private industry have probably noticed that there is a constant effort to improve business results over last year's business. Personal growth is a lifestyle, absolutely necessary.

I have heard it said Alexander The Great was a genius. I think, however, he was very much like all of humanity. He was perhaps like Thomas Edison, who claimed his genius was ninety percent sweat. Alexander just had confidence and courage; he understood his own potential, and the psychological nature of man. He was encouraged to think on his own. He had exactly what the youth of today do not have. We adults are their mentors. We have let them down. Who else could be responsible for how they learned to feel, think, and act. We are their coaches...

The books that can help students most are similar to the film "ET," they are both motivational and inspirational. Self-help books that focus on leadership and excellence can help students understand that there is hope and they do have ability. Understanding what successful people think and how they act will help them realize that they too can help solve some of the world's problems.

Almost everyone will pull himself or herself up to responsibility if given the power or authority to do so. Empowerment is like magic. The power of responsibility for your own learning, at least for one hour each day, can have a tremendous effect on how you feel about yourself.

Incidentally, all Peace Officers, who are closer than most of us to the real problems of youth, agree, self-esteem is the one thing children in trouble need.

Martin Luther King said, "The most important thing we can do for our children is help them believe in themselves." There is no reason, no excuse for our schools to continue ignoring practical thinking so necessary for daily living.

Education will remain a pleasure, instead of becoming a torture, if the spirit of exploration with an open, questioning, and adventurous mind is maintained.
—Anatole France

All of these very practical books, and many more, follow the same line of wisdom. It seems the number one thing they all mention is goal setting. They tell you reasons for setting goals, how to make plans and how to work your plans. They suggest you listen to your own gut feelings; if you have an obsession, you must follow it. They suggest that the plans must be written down. There is something magic about this. It helps crystallize and improve our thinking.

Creativity is also important; so you must use your imagination. Again, listen to your heart.

Most of the successful decisions I have made were made with my heart.
—Benjamin Netanyahu

Follow your hunches and your intuitive thinking. Be true to yourself, you have something special no one else has. Almost all books mention Socrates' famous aphorism, "Know thyself." They suggest, to understand yourself follow your curiosity, your natural talent— and maximize its use. Take a risk on your thinking and learn from your mistakes. We all have more talent than we use. We should renew and reinvent ourselves constantly.

Writers expand on words like: fear, mistakes, courage, faith, leadership, confidence, knowledge, listening, positive thinking, subconscious mind.

Many books discuss the use of affirmations that can be used to help us see the world in a positive way. They help us see both the freedom and responsibilities that come from thinking for ourselves. A steady diet of affirmations (See the quotations on Self Respect in Chapter Thirteen) can help us improve habits we would like to change.

Anyone who has used affirmations will agree, they do help change our thinking; but for some reason they are not part of our learning system. Are they too simple, too practical for the theory minded school administrators? I don't think so. The management of anything from a farm to a school needs a balance of crops or ideas.

If our schools had just one period of practical thinking, students would be more receptive to all other classes. Tough hardheaded discipline is a useful learning tool, but following you own enthusiasm, your own bliss can add a lot of interest to life. Self-reliance comes from learning through your own effort rather than being "taught" by a teacher. All of these books are written to encourage personal growth.

What am I getting at? Only this—practical thinking can change our world dramatically.

The Problem and the Cure

I suggest that students should think about, concentrate, and focus on knowledge of a subject that gives them personal growth. The daily feeling of moving ahead is critical. No one wants to spend his or her days in a nonproductive way. When we go to bed at night, there is nothing that replaces the statement; "I got a lot done today" or "I'll be stronger tomorrow, because of what I learned today."

I have had hundreds of one-on-one conversations with young men who say they absolutely go crazy sitting in class rooms where time is wasted and nonproductive 'work' is done. Tell me, are these kids crazy, or do our schools have a problem they are not aware of? If your first thought is that perhaps the kids are not able to judge whether the work they are doing is productive or not, how do you suggest they learn the distinction?

This reminds me of my experience in the retail business as a young man. My greatest fear was a customer who became a "silent walk away." These are customers who don't buy and don't say why. A good manager accepts the responsibility if this occurs. It is not the fault of the salespeople. Our schools don't have silent walk always, too many just go to jail; sometimes with a big bang.

Children need to be kept busy and it can't be busy work. We are so foolish when we assume they don't mind wasting their time. I suggest that students, everyday, write or rewrite personal essays that explain what they think on any subject they like.

Some of the great thinkers of all time have written essays that focus on just one-word subjects. Most of these essays were written and rewritten many times. There is no better way to learn; it forces the student to continue research, looking for additional information. The best way to improve learning, is to focus on a subject of high interest. The habit of focusing on one word can become self-education of your own design, taken to the student's personal measurement of excellence, judged only by the student. No teacher needs to read, evaluate or grade it.

Teachers can if a request is made, help the student find information. Carl R. Roger called it facilitation of learning.

Isn't It Strange, We Think The Same Thoughts Over and Over and Over: Release from the Endless Cycle

Thinking about writing and writing down one's thoughts creates a freedom that can be found no other way. Have you noticed, we often think the same thoughts over and over many times. Writing releases us from the endless cycle.

It creates a growing and learning situation; exactly what students need. *They will perhaps change their goal many times in their life, but a least, for today, they will know who they are and where they are going.* The feeling that they have learned something useful puts a little excitement in their life. Wisdom is not one of those things we slowly achieve; it comes with intentional effort, work we enjoy, and the fun we have learned to have with words.

Ideas You Can Use for an Active, Safe Community

Following is a list of authors and thinkers whose ideas can be put to use not only in the classroom setting but for adults and for whole communities. Though there are countless others, this is a list of some of the best of our contemporary thinkers: Jim Rohn, John C. Maxwell, William J. Bennett, Warren Bennis, Ken Blanchard, Jack Canfield, Dale Carnegie, Steven Covey, Peter F. Drucker, John W. Gardner, Bill Gates, Seth Godin, Mark Victor Hansen, Kets de Vries, C. William Pollard, Tom Peters, Faith Popcorn, Harvey McKay, Paul G. Stoltz, Dennis Waitley, Zig Ziglar.

I suggest if you read anyone of these writers you will find information you will find motivational and useful for your home or community.

CHAPTER 5

Leadership (pt2)

Winners Learn to Focus

An Olympic athlete is not a star without a great deal of effort. They must focus on their obsession. A diver has many techniques that must be learned. They must develop their own style from basics that have become a habit, with moves that are practiced over and over, hundreds of times. A gymnast, with the help of a coach, is actually practicing *self-education* techniques.

Most people can learn to swim, but some of us absolutely love swimming, so they are the ones who will naturally be the best swimmers. People excel in whatever they enjoy the most. A person who accomplishes anything worthwhile in life is a person who can focus and practice that same thing over and over.

Good examples are athletes, movie stars, and public speakers. Executives who manage large companies are actually teachers who repeatedly must focus the thinking of others. They constantly set and reset goals. They teach and teach, day after day. Most of all they help employees learn and practice focusing on first things, first. Learning to focus is an important habit that should be learned in school and at home.The habit of changing channels on the television does not improve this ability.

As mentioned before, I believe anyone can build a brick house, because the focus is with only one brick at a time. If you have the ability to focus on one brick, you can focus on one thousand, one at a time. Education can be built in the same way— one word at a time. It's easy to say, "I don't know what to focus on." The truth is, it makes no difference where you start, it only matters that you start; and that you be enthusiastic. Learning, changing, growing is well worthwhile.

Let's revisit Samuel Johnson's great quotation and apply it to the above paragraph: "It makes no difference, when you put pants on whether you put in the left or the right leg, Sir, you may stand disputing which is best to put in first, but in the meantime your backside is bare. Sir, while you stand considering which of two things you should teach your child first, another boy has learnt 'em both."

Pride and Respect

We do not have enough good teachers, and never will have enough to touch and inspire all those who are hungry for education. My self-education ideas can be adapted, with encouragement, to children in all schools; the younger the better.

My own education is based on simple words that interest me. At the age of sixteen my interest was management. I wanted to be the manager of a retail store. This interest expanded to other related words: communications, speaking, listening, psychology, philosophy, etc. I found that each word can be broken down into smaller parts; psychology for instance has many subtitles or specific areas of specialization. Some people spend their entire life studying one area; whatever happens to intrigue them.

As I grew older my words of interest became: love, marriage, parenting, children, education, self-respect. My interests grow and continue to change constantly. As previously mentioned I have a filing folder for every word of interest. They are full of notes I make and articles I cut out of magazines or copy from books.

My education is self-designed; no parent, teacher or counselor controls my thinking or my direction. I'm independent, my own man. I think, act, and follow through on what interests me most. My personal growth, my education is the result of keeping notes on all the great thoughts of successful people. It's the result of having read what others think and have thought, throughout history.

Our young people have no interest in history. No one knows what Columbus was thinking, how he felt in 1492. History books would be more exciting if written by Ray Bradbury or others who know what is important to the readers. And in fact, there are such books, that provide history and meaningful facts, written by talented writers who understand how to reach readers... but they don't show up in our classrooms.

Teenagers are suffering from lack of self-respect because they don't meet the standards set by adults in our schools.

It's difficult for me to imagine self-respect when someone else sets the goal. I don't believe it is possible.

The problem is, few adults listen carefully to young people before establishing goals. I have had so many tell me, "No one seems to care what we think." We need to compare the student's world with the real world. They see things we are missing.

But things are different when the shoe is on the other foot. In the adult world of work, adults are demanding that they be allowed to put in their two-cents worth. They want to help plan the work and improve the work that is being done. They have often been known to sabotage the boss's goals if they are considered only a puppet that does exactly what they are told.

I realize there is no one cure for our education system, so I offer only one suggestion. My hope is that all schools will allow students to follow their own curiosity the first period of every school day. It should be a time for creativity. It is an ideal time for students to write their own book; this book can become a lifetime of good habits and information.

If a student will search and find solutions to their own problems they will enjoy and appreciate the discovery more than any other way. A student's book should be a summary of self- knowledge and discovery initiated independently. It can be an up to date record of what today's thinking is. It helps them "know thyself" and it helps the student like what they see when they look in the mirror.

The most creative time for most people is early morning; it is an ideal time to express what they think and feel. Students will learn more from writing their own book than from any other way. It will give some balance to their day, making it easier for them to tolerate teaching methods that are necessary for some classes.

It will also put some creativity into their day. Creativity is what makes our day, everyday of our life. Successful fulfillment of life is not possible without work and creativity. It is the essence of life and the beginning of personal wisdom. Self-respect and pride develops spontaneously from "Your own creation—a book with your own design." We all need to learn how to express ourselves. We can grow from our expressions; have renewed faith in ourselves and also in our discoveries. It's a learning process that makes us better tomorrow, because of what we learn today.

Self-expression will improve student ability to survive and excel in all other classes. It will create a twenty-four hour habit of individualistic thinking...personal growth at its best. This is an easy way for students to pursue an interest that will arouse their curiosity. To keep it simple and make it easier to focus on learning, only one word should describe the subject. I suggest that students as a learning process do their own research. They should find all the information they can on each word they have a personal interest in. We often don't know what we think until we speak or write it down.

Students who fail in school often say, "These classes are not relevant." The opportunity to follow what they think relevant, at least one period a day, will renew excitement for learning. It will create respect for learning in many new areas of their life.

I believe this book of their own is a practical way to explore their own thinking. It is a new way to find what Socrates thought important: To know thyself. The habits students develop here will become a lifetime interest in learning. It will help them continuously renew and reinvent themselves on a daily basis.

It was William James who said that most men are old fogies at twenty-five because they have ceased to grow. Dr. Elijah P. Brown suggested that the man who is not always in school, trying to learn something from everything and everybody, will soon be dried up and stored away with the other mummies.

People Don't Respect Our Youth, So They Prove Us Right

I don't know how this happened, but there seems to be a lack of honesty within us. We seem to know what we are doing is wrong, but we as a society are unable to act. Fear is probably what holds us back. What I mean is, we have intuitive hunches, desires, goals, even dreams, but we just don't listen to ourselves. We don't act spontaneously, childlike; instead we act-out what we think is mature, controlled. We stifle our potential, we disappoint ourselves; we stumble and fall, clearly getting in the way of our own goals.

Work is enjoyed when we are doing what we love. School and learning is enjoyed for the same reason; because we think what we are doing is important and fun.

A student who is honest and has self-respect does not learn because they want to please someone else. If they are being true to themselves, how can they enjoy what someone else thinks is important?

Where is the excitement, the commitment, the burning desire that says, "I'm doing the most important thing in my life, right now?" Everyone has a different feeling, a different interest; a desire to-doodle-fiddle-and play in their own way.

Commitment comes from an obsession that's burning with intensity on the inside. It's a natural curiosity that takes our interest off everything else. It makes us forget time and where we are. We are at this moment exactly where we want to be.

Children are at their best when their energy, curiosity, and commitment explode without effort. Efficiency and naturalness will thrive, when learning, work and play-flows like a river, finding its own way.

Both teachers and parents, without realizing it, have a tendency to silence the power within; the vigorous desire we all have to fulfill ourselves. This misuse of natural energy humiliates our young people and deteriorates our communities. Crime and drug use is caused by misdirected energy. Lack of education is the reason. Lack of leadership is the cause. Self-education is the cure. Self-education is without cost, yet it is the most effective learning process.

We Are Individuals First

I don't like to take on the role of a preacher, but it's important that we take an honest look at ourselves. We are all individuals, not teams, groups, or gangs. We are, strong or weak, the total make-up of our community.

If we are strong individuals, our communities will find that same strength. We are interrelated, we affect each other like a chain that is as strong as its weakest link, but we are also individuals who can pull each other up.

Our so-called leaders should help both individuals and communities find and maximize potential. History will show eventually that our education problems will be solved, but we need to focus on the problem, now. Democracy works, there is no doubt in my mind, but its reaction to problems is sometimes slow.

Failure of Mass Education

This book is not attempting to teach. My purpose is to make information available so it's possible to design your own education. Students' own thoughts should guide the direction of their own learning. It should not be something a so-called expert thinks students should believe or study.

As I have mentioned, while working for the California Youth Authority I tried to convince my supervisors that Dale Carnegie's *How To Win Friends and Influence People* should be the backbone of our rehabilitation program. It was considered, at that time the best selling book of all time, except for the Bible.

I have since discovered that when Aristotle was teaching Alexander The Great he used similar practical techniques. He did not believe that what we call academic subjects should be taught until Alexander had self-respect, a set of internal values that would later make academic subjects easily mastered. He apparently liked Socrates famous quote: "Know thyself."

As far as I know Dale Carnegie's book has never been used in a classroom setting. Our education leaders in the past forty years have chosen not to be as practical as Aristotle. I think we should question the value of their advice.

Good management usually requires effective listening to clients and history. Most of those who have a Ph.D. appear to be following each other; they make a simple problem into a complex one. Working with committee mentality they help us analyze the analysis of the analysis. Life and its activities are not as complex as they make them out to be. It seems to me there is now an even greater need for us to understand and respect our own individuality. We seem, today, to be fascinated with the computer, but it will never replace the human mind.

Socrates' "Know-thyself" statement is more valuable than ever. Parents and teachers need to dwell on this thought. If we lack self-respect, we may as well throw-in-the-towel.

We can learn on our own, without being totally controlled by family, friends and teachers.

Our world is as large as our courage and as interesting as our thoughts. No book is an end in itself, so the value of a conclusion is doubtful. We should not come to a conclusion that appears to be set in concrete. We should instead be open minded and curious about everything.

A conclusion takes us to the end of our search for wisdom, a tragic ending. If we conform to everyone's thinking; if a lack of excitement for learning continues, life is going to be very dull; especially for those of us who like to learn and grow.

Science, if it continues without conclusions set in concrete, will in the future solve problems we are not aware of today. Democracy, with its freedom for people, should remain open to new problems. If it does, personal growth of individuals and society will continue to be exciting. The search for knowledge, the possibilities for life on this planet, are endless.

Here is one problem that concerns me. I pray that we do not become so scientific that we forget that people and the common sense they provide will be our only way of keeping this world habitable; a safe place to live.

Even today I recommend Dale Carnegie's book. It has been a basic requirement for all successful business managers for the last forty years. One idea he provides his readers with is that no one ever wins an argument. I'm convinced you should not argue with me. Read the book. It should be required reading for all high school students. Social skills are their most valuable lifetime tool.

We Are Not Listening to Our Great Teachers

Montaigne's thinking on "The Education of Children," though written long ago, can still serve today as a guideline of sorts. It was written in the 1500s. I have several of his quotes under the headline of education, but I highly recommend that you buy his essays and make notes of your own on every page. It will improve your own education and give you, as Samuel Johnson said,"some new lights on education."

I am about to do something a professional writer would never do. (Lucky, as noted, I consider myself an amateur, and so enjoy the freedoms that such a title affords.) I want to repeat a quotation

I think clearly identifies reasons for some of the pain we have recently suffered because of teenage frustration. I totally believe we adults are not doing the right thing for our kids. They need to know their life is going to be a great and successful adventure. I've seen the tears. I can feel the sorrow. Yet, I believe there has never been a better time to be young. This is one of my favorite quotations from Montaigne: *I agree with Plutarch, that Aristotle did not waste his great pupil's time on lessons in the construction of syllogisms, or on the principle of geometry, but taught him wise precepts on the subject of valor, prowess, magnanimity, temperance, and that assurance which knows no fear.*

In other words he did not teach rules of logic and deduction, or the principles of geometry, but taught him wise rules on the subject of courage, physical skills, to think "big" about himself and that he could make a difference in the world. He taught him to be noble and if necessary heroic. He taught him to think on a grand scale, with strength and power of his own design. Personal self-restraint was an important lesson. He taught him ambition, generosity, forgiveness, liberalism, and tolerance. He taught him to be comfortable with himself; to have hope, confidence and belief in himself. Self-respect was important, with a self-assurance that knows no fear. His student felt a flexible competence, useful, optimistic; he felt himself to be an important part of the world. He felt like Alexander the Great!

A Note to Teachers

I can understand that you may ask yourself; who am I to be giving a teacher advice. Let me tell you a story. There was a very successful restaurant owner who claimed his success came from inspection of trashcans at his dishwashing area. He checked everything that was thrown in the trash. If there was a quality problem it had to be the seasoning. It could also be the hot food was not hot or cold food was not cold. He always wanted to know, Why?

I lived in the trashcan, the prison system, of our society eight to sixteen hours a day for twenty years. I have literally asked the question "Why?" thousands of times. My claim to fame has been, "I am the world's best listener." No one has challenged me on this; they just call me "Pops" and keep on talking. Their comment was: "Mr. E. really cares, I can't believe this guy."

They did not know that I left home at the age of fourteen, and because my experience, I was very much like them; I could read their mind. I had been there and done that. I was a certified juvenile delinquent who could see their problem and help them, in their words, "pull their head out."

Successful education listens to the students' gut feelings. Each student has a built in intuitive interest, an excitement that needs some straight talk. They called it B.S.; I called Heifer Dust. You need to get down to their level if you want to hear honest thinking come to life; the kind they love to share with a good listener.

An adult's too-serious, often dogmatic intentions actually stifle the human instinct; that instinct which in children is a desire to act on their own thinking. We foolishly think a tough, disciplined approach, with back to basics thinking is correct for our children. We need to reexamine and soften our approach. It is only partially correct, not, a total solution. Freedom to learn what students want to learn for a one hour period of time each day needs consideration. *It can become the habit of learning to accept responsibility.* We all enjoy having responsibility; too many of us have not yet had the pleasure, or made the discovery.

We adults pretend to be so mature, so all wise and knowing; we are officiously digging the educational grave of our children. Our frustration, confusion, and insecurity are causing us to be controllers rather than self-sufficient, confident facilitators of learning.

Self-education is nothing new; our recent educators have just failed to focus on history. The power of self-education can be found in almost any autobiography. Read: Jefferson, Lincoln, Franklin, Edison, Henry Ford, Martin Luther King, Eleanor Roosevelt,

Florence Nightingale, Virginia Woolf, etc. The list goes on and on.

My own writing technique and purpose, as far as I know is different than any used in the past. Teachers have often tried to use a journal or diary for their students; most teachers have given up on the idea because students eventually use it as a form of manipulation. They write what they think the teacher or parent wants to hear, or something that will give a good impression.

This kind of writing quickly becomes non-productive.

A student's writing should focus on personal growth and honesty compared only with what they used to think. They should be made aware of the fact that their thinking will change. An essay on love or marriage from any author today will be different one year from now, if they are learning anything from their life's experience.

Part of their learning should be without competition; not compared with the performance of other students. Their learning process should constantly move to new ideas and the thinking goal should be simple; just one word. Self-education requires being honest with one's self. Being candid, open and honest brings out the best in all of us. In my own case, I follow what my interests are. I hear words all day long that cause me to wonder: *What can I learn now?* I either make a mental note of the thought, or write it down before I lose it.

There is absolutely no way to grow without specific concentration on what interests you most. You can't say, "I want wisdom." It is a general statement without focus. You must religiously focus on your curiosity. But, you must also realize and expect that your thinking and opinions will change as you find new information.

If Education Were a Business, Costs Would be Analyzed

…And grading papers would have to prove its value. If a business can change, grow, and get better every year, so can our education system. We need to ask ourselves questions that create results. For example: What is the most important activity in a business situation? Accounting, always. Who is the most productive person in business? The salesman. No sales, no business. What does the modern salesman of today focus on? Service, first, last, and always.

This kind of thinking can be applied to the school grading system. If grades become too important the student will lose interest. If the student loses interest there is no learning.

All the grading systems in the world will not improve learning. My thinking is that an intentional, optimistic focus on learning will generate high learning. In business positive action is focused on the most productive, activity. It is the source of the most profit. The focus is on the positive, not the negative. Nothing can replace sales. Nothing will replace intense focus on the word courage until you consider yourself an expert, or another interest comes to your attention.

If education were a business, grading papers would have to prove it has value. Smart business people are ruthless— when costs are unnecessary, they cut costs immediately. My question is, can you prove the grading system is improving the results? My own experience taught me massive action during the Christmas season creates more profit in one day than one week any other time of the year.

Massive action on the most important activity is a must. Tough-minded focus on results leaves no room for sissies who would rather count the stars in the sky. Intensity, commitment, focus will create maximum profit. in the next hour, day, week, month, and year. Goals should be reduced to smaller achievable goals and reevaluated constantly.

I'm suggesting grading papers should not be given more importance than it deserves. It is quite possible the time teachers spend correcting papers could be used to design creative ways to shake up the students; to get them out of the rut they are in; to create learning excitement, to give students the kind of responsibility they love. The possibilities are endless. The great need is focus and intention.

Grading papers is not motivational. Does the experience cause any student to smile, or jump with joy? It does not improve enthusiasm for learning. If we think about all of the positive things created since the beginning of time, in every situation the inventor's thinking was positive. Thinkers of all kinds who had an obsession and a dream knew how to get the job done. Yet, critics who say it can't be done usually surround them. Expecting results or success is in every situation the key to success. Henry Ford believed, "If you think you can, you can." "Corrected," sometimes called, "critical thinking," would have prevented invention of the telephone and use of electricity. The world is full of negative people who think you are foolish to try something you have never done before.

Teachers who point out errors do not create excitement for learning. This horrible negative approach in classrooms may easily be part of the reason why teenagers need a gun in their hand. A gun makes them a capable person!! Juveniles want attention; if it is good, or if it is bad, it is still attention. This is sad but true, it proves, very much like pain that they are alive. Teenagers want to be a part of the same activity their friends enjoy.

I know without question that red correction marks are destructive to a child who already has a low self-image. If we do not have a better way to improve the learning process we need to invent one. Time spent analyzing the correction of papers needs serious attention. We need to ask ourselves the following questions:

—Can teachers prove correcting papers in all situations is time well spent?

—Is correction equally valuable in mathematics, science, English, history, etc?

—Does time spent correcting papers cost taxpayers too much?

—Is there a subject where occasional correction would prove valuable?

—Is correction based on fear students are not learning?

—Is enthusiasm more valuable than fear as a learning tool?

—Can students help with, and learn from helping with the correction process?

—Would our faith and confidence in youth increase their ability to learn how to learn?

—Would an Efficiency Management Consultant approve of time spent correcting papers?

—Can a teacher effectively teach fifty students rather than twenty if students correct their own papers?

—How many more evaluation-questions can we ask ourselves about grading papers?

Ken Blanchard, in his book *The Heart Of A Leader* describes an unusual teaching experience.

He gave his students the final test on the first day of school. Everyday he wandered around the classroom interacting with feedback from his students. Student goals were very clear. All students got an A.

Would such creative teaching reduce the need for the task of correcting papers?

CHAPTER 6

Self Improvement

Listen to Yourself; Respect Yourself

I often tell young people that the most important thing they can do while young is to find their obsession. I suggest, find what interests you most, and then follow it in every way possible. They usually look at me, confused, and say, "How do I find my obsession, I don't even know what I want to do tomorrow?"

My answer is:

"It's easy." It's easy because, all that is needed is to follow your own thinking; the secret is in your daily thoughts.

The trick is to write down your thoughts. The first thought, like a good idea, is a seed that will grow if given the freedom and encouragement needed. I believe you must be openly honest with yourself and open to criticism without being defensive. You need to prove nothing to anyone but yourself, so listen to advice from others, but respect your own judgment.

If your thoughts are given the respect they deserve, by recording them in written form, your mission in life will clearly identify itself. The difficult part of this process, is the discipline required to write every day.

Richard V. Eastman

I'd like to convince young people in my community, that those who write down their thinking discover their potential, those who don't won't; it's that simple. Writing what you think is like magic, it will clarify what Socrates thought important, "Know thyself."

A student's success depends on the ability to be an honestly and totally transparent person. "What you see is what you get." No phonies allowed! We are all different; there is a need to find our own niche, talent or purpose in life. I often suggest, study the nature of man. There is nothing wrong with imitating qualities you see in other people. We all have our heroes.

A good example of a perfect human being is an infant. They listen to their body and react spontaneously to what they think and feel. They are learning at a fantastic speed because they have not yet allowed themselves to be controlled by parents, teachers and counselors.

Society stifles the normal development of most of us. If we could remain childlike in many ways we would eventually develop our own potential. The one word we hear more than any is: No, No, No. How do you find success when you have been repeatedly told it can't be done?

Don't Repeat Yourself

Bryan said, "I read thirty minutes everyday for the purpose of waking up my mind." He wrote because he had thoughts that needed to be put down on paper. Many great thinkers believed the best ways to learn were to write down their thoughts. The process gives enlightenment and depth.

There is something magic, something happens, on the inside, when you say what is in your heart and on your mind. We all, some of us don't realize it, have a need to give the world our two-cents worth, even if the world does not read it. It feels good to say what is on your mind. The process of learning is improved by comparing our thoughts, with that of others.

Brenda Ueland had some thinking on this. She said, "Blake thought that creative power should be kept alive in all people, all of their lives." And so do I. Why? Because it is life itself. It is the Spirit. In fact it is the only important thing about us. The rest of us is legs and stomach, materialistic craving and fears. How could we keep it alive: By using it, by letting it out, by giving some time to it.

Everyone has the same bad habits when it comes to thinking. We think the same thoughts, over and over and over. This stops our own personal growth. It prevents learning something new. It keeps us from moving on to the next thought or a new idea.

I have been my own worst enemy; but, it is a bad habit I have been able to change, and so will you. Writing down my thoughts clears my mind immediately. Gridlock is over, my mind continues on. I like to keep moving in some direction, even if it is wrong.

Action inevitably invents something new; either a different problem or a solution to an old one. We can learn something new everyday. You may even begin to think that wisdom is on the way...getting closer every day!

I have a personal motto that says: "I want to be a better man tomorrow because of what I learn today."

I could say that I am obsessed with learning, but not just for the sake of learning. I want to be more effective as a person. I want to make a difference in the world. It seems like a good philosophy for all of us. Maybe this is our purpose in life.

Certainly you have more potential than you are using! We find more satisfaction, real happiness, as you begin to discover and use the best part of our, as yet, unused potential. Happiness, the fun, is in the searching. It's the discovery of something new, something you did not know, about the nature of things, or about yourself.

Writing seems to crystallize your thought. It takes us somewhere we haven't been before. It brings out new thoughts and opinions that have been in hiding all this time.

New Recipes Cook Up New Success

My method of learning is a kind of mechanical system for filing away my thinking. It's a foundation, a building foundation for new ideas that have not yet made an appearance in my life. Your own methods of learning depends on your ability to collect new recipes, new thoughts, and new ideas.

"You become what you eat and you become what you think, so you are whatever you have an interest in."

That's the key, I think, to develop as many interests as possible.

You become interesting to yourself and to others by having many things that you are curious about.

It may seem possible to watch hundreds of hours of television with the expectation of finding a useful education; it doesn't work that way. Television is a passive learning process. It may shape your attitude in many ways, but useful learning will not come from television unless you are a politician who wants to impress others with how much you care.

Current affairs will make no difference in your life unless you want to entertain your friends. Personal entertainment should take-up only ten-percent of your time. Life is not a spectator sport. The knowledge you have must be acted on or it has no value. Ten college degrees have no value unless the knowledge is creating a profit or making life better in the big city.

Learn From Your Own Thinking

Your education should be on what interests you. Fun in learning is to have an education of your own design. You will enjoy going where your thoughts and curiosity take you. Why bother with anything else? If you want to discipline yourself, something we all need occasionally, it should be focused on a subject you want to know more about. I ask you seriously, what is more important than what you think? It can't be what others think unless you want to imitate them. I'm reminded of a quotation I found somewhere: "I learned the important thing is not what others think of me, but what I think of me."

There is, of course, a problem with independent thinking; you may be considered a rebel. Our education system has not yet reached the point where it can help us follow our own interest or potential. Teachers want us to think what they want us to think. I call it: "The old-controlling-teacher syndrome." It's crazy, it's like spinning your wheels in the mud, it's non-productive, inefficient; it's a waste of human energy, commitment, and enthusiasm.

My purpose in life is to find what I'm good at, to answer my own questions and work the hell out of any special ability I have. The remaining years of my life will be spent making as many mistakes as I can crowd into each hour. Wisdom, the all-inclusive search for purpose in life, is found only from our own mistakes. I cannot give you wisdom, nor can you give me mine; but, we can stay connected.

> *Men are polished,*
> *through act and speech*
> *Each by each,*
> *As pebbles are smoothed*
> *on the rolling beach.*
> *With years a richer life begins,*
> *The spirit mellows:*
> *Ripe age gives tone to violins,*
> *wine, and good fellows.*
> —*John T. Trowbridge*

I repeat, at the risk of sounding like a preacher; most or should I say too many parents and teachers suffer from what I call "controlitis." They want students to be tough and disciplined with the back to basics movement, which they think is right for them. They don't seem to realize that they are shoveling sand against the tide.

Everything in the world has a natural bent, a natural inclination to go its own way. If a student has a natural interest, a talent, and a curiosity in some direction, they should follow it in every way possible. Peter Drucker has a point that we should consider. He said, "Good management requires that talent and ability should be maximized."

Character or a good team is built on the use of positive, not negative people and situations. If you are a person who is not following your imagination, ideas, intuition, you are wasting valuable time.

Of course, I realize that we all need self-discipline; and that we need some hills to climb, some problems to solve. It builds character and a toughness that is useful, but a good balance is needed. We would still be reading by candlelight if Thomas Edison had been forced to study literature. He is a good example of a man who followed his own natural inclinations.

"We Need Self Respect"

I'm concerned with young people who do not have the confidence and self-respect they deserve. It's not their fault; it's a responsibility we adults have failed to develop. We have not listened to the great teachers of the past. I really don't understand, actually it makes no difference whose fault it is or how it happened; our schools have lost touch with reality. They are not, along with parents, giving our children what they need most, and that is self-respect.

Emerson said, "If you must teach a child, give them respect." (I wonder, is he implying that we are incompetent teachers or that the child may learn more on its own ?)

Because we adults suffer from "controlitis," and we consider ourselves the great authority figure, we fail to listen to those who really know, our children! Our schools will continue to fail as long as we are not listening.

I've mentioned before, teaching a child is similar to training a race-horse.

Too much discipline takes all the fun out of running your own race. Our children need a free rein to experiment with their brain. Self-respect is not a gift from someone else; we earn it because of our own activities.

Samuel Johnson said, "I believe courage and intellect the two qualities best worth a good mans cultivation."

This ties in very well with my own thinking; wisdom is what I need most! I'm still searching. I find a small amount of self-respect each day.

Socrates believed that to "know thyself," to discover our ability is important to successful living. Life has been better for myself since I have learned to think about myself in a positive way. Self-respect is available for anyone who takes a good look at themselves. Potential and possibilities are always there. We need to use ourselves, to experience ourselves. Action can be the cause of us jumping into water when we cannot swim; if this happens we become resourceful, we learn to swim in any way we can. This builds strength and character; action is the catalyst that creates personal growth. "When the going gets tough, the tough get going."

Montaigne wrote: "I study myself more than any other subject. This is my metaphysics; this is my natural philosophy."

I constantly search myself for natural ability, for things I am good at. I have discovered that most people, including myself, usually find what they are looking for.

Abraham Lincoln said: "Most folks are as happy as they make up their minds to be."

If I continuously look for good things about myself, I can find them. In fact, that is really all I'm looking for. I've heard and seen enough of my faults. My focus is positive when ever possible.

Suggestion for teenagers: Make a list of one hundred things you like about your self. *Strength creates strength.* A football coach once told me that if a team had a good offense, in other words, good running and passing action, defensiveness has a less important role. I believe life is very much like a football game;

being defensive tends to reduce or stifle the freedom and joy of living. I would rather reach for the gold, take a risk and fail if necessary. I want action, not inaction.

Goethe believed that his most important life work was to discover and expand his own talent.

I have found that I can do almost anything if I decide that I want to do it. It's just a matter of concentration. My attitude is that I want to do this job better than anyone has ever done it before. I don't always succeed, but I find that it's fun trying. If I have done the job before I always try to improve on my last performance. I don't expect perfection, but I like giving it my "best shot."

Follow the Bouncing Ball

You will find that if you follow the action of a bouncing ball, it will take you places you do not expect. That's also the nature of self-education. If a student has the courage to follow their own interests their education will focus its self. Tell yourself: "I'm following my own instinct, my intuition, because I want to know where it is going to take me next."

Thomas Edison supposedly did this ten thousand times. Candles are no longer necessary because of his persistent self-education. He followed his own thinking. So, teachers, ONE HOUR a day, ask your students to pick a word, any word, and follow where it takes them. They will be surprised how many interests they have and how interesting they have become to both themselves and others.

Friend or teacher cannot design true self-respect. It is an internal activity; a rumble of action and energy from its own fuel...curiosity and enthusiasm...a mighty force that needs no explanation.

I have found three words high school age students have a special interest in. They are: *confidence, courage, feelings*; let them look to their heroes first, for meaning. Next, let them skim, read or study the thinking of any famous person that intrigues them. Their research will invent an essay, which will be rewritten many times through the years.

Self-Education Is Not for Sissies

You must be a "tough-son-of-a-gun." You must love a good fight. You must be competitive by fighting against your own last performance. Today, after your daily activities, you should read five hours. You may not be able to do this every night, but it should be your intention. Your physical goal should be to develop the muscle between your ears; your expectations should not be too easy. If it is, you are not working hard enough. If it is too easy you are not testing yourself, you have not given yourself a challenge that is worthy of you. You can reach higher; you can do better. It's very much like lifting weights; if you try harder you can lift that weight one more time. If you are running, you can run one more mile. Talk to yourself; say, "I can do it, I can do it."

Focus, focus, focus; keep your eye on the ball. A highly motivated, aggressive player doesn't always know what to focus on, but they concentrate on something. An athlete, while training, finds a muscle that has not been over used. They give exercise where it is needed. All muscles must be strong. Don't try to be scientific so every decision is perfect; it can't be done, just create some action, start anywhere, now!

Keep the ball bouncing, eventually you will be an amateur with many interests; have a liberal education, or be a rocket scientist. You will find, you are more interesting to yourself and to others. Look up the word tough in the dictionary and Roget's Thesaurus. Look for quotations on ability, determination, energy, firmness, strength, resolution, etc. There is power in your knowledge of strength and action.

Visualize Intellectualism

If you are going to focus on brainpower, that famous muscle between your ears, you must visualize yourself as a high performer. Successful athletes can visualize themselves performing during their highest and best performance. At the beginning of there training session they are not at their best, but as Napoleon Hill suggested:

"If you can see it, and believe it, you will achieve it."

Visualize yourself as a person with brainpower. I don't mean to be immodest, but I believe you must see your self as an intellectual. You must believe you have the power to solve problems successfully. This confidence that you visualize will make it so. Designing your own education is like learning to swim: dive in the water, not too deep, and begin to paddle, stay above the water any way that you know how. But again, you must focus on a specific part of your learning process. Begin with a word that you have an interest in. To show you how, I'11 pick a word for you.

Let's start with the word courage.

What do you know about courage? Answer the questions: What? Where? How? What is courage? Experiment with the word; define it in every way possible. When is a person courageous? Where is courage possible? If you can find some examples, write them down. How can you be courageous? Learning about anything requires that you know its history. You must know what people think and have thought about courage. You should either agree or disagree with their thinking. This is now your chance wrestle and discuss with others, what is right or wrong.

You need to develop some opinions, but remember, they often change with new information. You can't stand tall; you can't express your self unless you have given it some "thinking time." Let it wake you up in the middle of the night.

Find some solitude each day to think about courage. Next month you can focus on a different word.

Write It Down, Write It Down, Write It Down

If you don't write it down you will be thinking about it—day after day—in the same way, with the same words, six months from now. Think about this—are you boring? I hope not!

Don't do that to yourself. It wastes you, your talent, ability, and time. You don't have time to waste. Use your time well, in every way, every day. Find everything your brain has to offer on this subject. Dig deep, get it out on paper so you can really see it; it becomes real when you can see your words on paper. If you want to have fun with words you should read, in fact, all teenagers should read this book ten times. I'm not kidding: *Zen in the Art of Writing by* Ray Bradbury. It has, incidentally, absolutely nothing to do with religion.

I have a habit of writing my thoughts down immediately before they slip my mind. If I don't get them while they are hot they may never return. There are times when we think the same thoughts over and over. This prevents personal growth. As soon as we write down our thought, we have released ourselves.

We are free to move on to something else which builds and expands on yesterday's thinking. Our growth depends on new and changing thoughts. We need to complete our thinking on yesterday's subject so we can improve, add to it, or move on to a different subject. *No one else has control of the words that you put on paper.*

It's a special kind of freedom, done "My way," a personal choice. The habit of writing what we think and feel becomes the direction of life we live. We follow our own thoughts, they always come before the actual activity. Carl Lewis had to first "think" he could be a fast runner before he created the action that took him to his final success. Our written thoughts lead us to our goals, our success, and a true picture of what our life is going to be.

My own personal writing is divided into two areas. One is an attempt to unload my brain everyday. Call it therapy if you like. I solve most of my problems through physical exercise or with writing; they are both my FREEDOM and GROWTH process. The other reason for writing is to gather ideas that intrigue me. I am constantly looking for new knowledge; the goal is wisdom. I may never find it, but the search is wonderful. Unloading my brain requires only pencil and paper. It's a simple process of writing down every thought that comes to my mind.

If you want to try it I suggest you set aside ten minutes of time. Write as fast as you can; your fingers will get tired, but keep on writing. If your thought is, "I can't think of anything to write." Write it down. Anything, it makes no difference what comes to your mind, just get it down. If you will do this every night, you will soon find that it's the best part of your day.

Creative Reading

My learning has come from my own books; I buy both new and old books. Most of them are used books that I pay fifty cents to two dollars for. I don't like to read a book unless I can make notes on every page. My time is too valuable; there are too many books to read for the sake of entertainment. I have never read a book without adding to my warehouse of knowledge.

The most valuable reading you can do is to read what you have written. I suggest create small essays for several of your favorite words. Examples: Confidence, courage, creativity, education, goals, individualism, leadership, listening, love, mistakes, optimism, responsibility, self-respect, etc. These essays will help you think about purpose, and intention: what you think yourself to be, what you believe, and who you want to be. Rereading and rewriting it will change and improve your thinking each time you read it. Rewrite it once a month or when ever you hear someone famous using the word. You will be surprised how your thinking changes when you focus on your favorite words.

My books are literature, philosophy, psychology, education, management, leadership, religion and many others. I like essays and stories about people; they are usually full of ideas that explain how they think and feel. I usually read a book in the normal way; but my focus is only on what is of interest to me.

My attitude is, the author did his or her thing, now I'll do mine. I don't have to follow the layout or the way the ideas are presented. I'm looking for what I want, not what the writer thinks I should have.

I call this creative reading. Each book is different, however; sometimes it is necessary to follow their thinking because one idea leads to the next. Most of the time I get bored with the development of their ideas. I may read the conclusion first. Sometimes I begin in the middle and look both ways for ideas.

To me, it's like eating a bunch of grapes. I always eat the best one first. They are my grapes. My purpose also, is to change the writer's ten-dollar words into twenty-five cent words. I'm not impressed with a Ph. D., who is trying to impress us with his vocabulary; besides I may only understand one sentence on each page. I never read a book that is easy to read; what is the use? I want to stretch my ability to think new thoughts. I usually skim a book looking for ideas. If the book is good I may read it two or three times.

My note keeping system, as far as I know, is a new idea. I can skim the average book in one hour. My purpose is to find what "works" for me. The interest can be defined with one word. A good example is the word courage. I can turn pages at a rapid speed and find the word courage every time. There is however a problem with this. I often find a sentence that refers to courage without using the word.

I have found that every thought I have can be placed in a one-word category. If my thought is about mother, children, marriage, education, management, whatever; I use that word as the subject index to file the quotation.. Sometimes a quotation can be placed under more than one category. For instance, I have the same quotation filed under courage, goals, and leadership. My one word index, of all my interests have made it possible for me to read almost any page in a book, magazine or newspaper, with profit.

I find little bits of wisdom everywhere. I use my words of interest as a tool to hang my education on. I can read a book about management and find information on marriage. I can read about love and find information on leadership. My word index helps me design my own education.

To finish the process of making the book all mine, I create my own index on the inside of the front cover. Every word-subject that begins with the letter A to K is listed on the first blank page, inside the cover. Words that begin with letters L to Z are on the second page. Example: Information I have found in the book on the word courage can be found on pages 10, 12, 20, 22, 31, 32, etc. If the quotation or idea is outstanding I circle the page number. This index is my memory bank; it is the source of all ideas I like to save. If I want information on the word courage I can look through several books and find information on courage. Complete information on my interests are quickly available inside of the front cover of all my books.

To broaden learning I suggest that students read poetry, humor, quotations, and essays at every opportunity. All of us are empty shallow people unless we fill our toolbox with thoughts and ideas from people who have had a different experience than our own. We can learn from mistakes others share with us.

The Value of Quotations

Most of what I have been able to learn about poetry indicates that poets use the most effective words available. They use words that express, the most that can be said, in the least number of words. It's true I think that a few strong words can inspire or change people's thinking dramatically. The purpose of speech or writing is to be efficiently persuasive. It appears to be true that fewer words have more power. There is a problem with poetry, which happens to be my own personal problem. The fact is, I don't understand a great deal of poetry. I wish I did. It is a problem I am working on; and it is a problem I intend to solve, because some poetry does give me pleasure. I often like the sound of the words; sometimes I just like the topic because it is something I am in the mood for. Usually, however it does not give back as much as I expect for the investment of time required. I'm a very practical guy; my time is important to me, so I value how I spend it.

Quotations, however, are a better use of words and time. The rewards I receive are almost immediate. They have meaning and purpose. They expose common sense ideas that are useful.

People who are quotable are usually very good at what they do. They are serious, sincere and want to help others. They want to share what they have found to be true. Their words are usually a gift, given freely, with no strings attached or thanks expected. Successful people have found a way to be both efficient and practical. Whatever they may have to say about a subject has credibility and is worth consideration.

If it were possible to be scientific about words, quotations would be "scientifically speaking" the most efficient learning tool available. They are usually spoken by the expert of the day, with power and conviction. So, the study of quotations should be taken seriously by anyone who wants to learn. I like to put quotations in categories that simplify my thinking. I want only an education of my own design, so the collection of enough quotations can help development of opinions on my subject of interest.

Thomas Edison had the habit of looking for practical information. He read every book on each shelf where he found an interest. The library was his tool. If you can broaden your experience with quotations like Thomas Edison did with a thousand books, your problems and dreams will find their own solutions.

The trick is to develop as many interests as possible. Having more recipes in the back of your mind will help you cook up a broader range of success. I suggest as you develop confidence on any subject, that you write a small essay that explains your up to the minute opinions. You will find as time goes by, you will want to change your essay because of new information. Your essay will get better improve with age. Your learning will be more interesting and your growth will be obvious.

"It is a good thing for an educated man to read books of quotations."
Sir Winston Churchill

Write Your Personal Philosophy

One of my lifetime philosophies is: I want to spend the rest of my life doing what is fun, exciting, and even scary. Writing is the safest risk you can take; yet it has the most rewards. No one has to read what you have written, but it will help you realize what you think about any subject you write on. It will clarify your dreams and help establish goals.

Writing is action without action until you are ready to send what you think to the local editor or the governor. Writing down your thoughts will force you to grow. It will make you a more successful parent or help you in any career you chose. I want to take risks that challenge me, and I want to make as many mistakes as possible. *Mistakes are the most powerful learning experience we can have.*

The truth is, with the exception of your religious belief, there really is no such thing as security in this life. Life is an open book with a beginning and an end. Risk is everywhere. It's where the fun in life is. Whatever happens between youth and old age depends upon how successful you are at finding the genius you have been given. It's your lifetime job to find and use up all that has been given you.

No one really knows what his or her potential is. People who "stand out" are those who risk the possibility that they may be wrong. They have the courage to try and keep on trying; they never give up on the quality of their own thinking.

Everyone's life reflects a philosophy of safety and security, or risk and courage. If you don't care where you go or don't know where you want to go, your direction makes no difference. Go anyway!

Action is more important than direction. Your many interests, what ever you learn, will eventually surprise you with a mission, an obsession. Personal growth, because of action, will flood you with many avenues of fulfillment.

Create Action

In my search for wisdom I constantly look of a way to create action that is useful. I look for a problem I can solve without procrastination. I like a challenge, something I know I can do. I believe we need to live right now, this moment, every day. Life is better when we are free and open to all things. (Legal, moral, and nonfattening.)

I don't pretend, fret or attempt to jump out of my skin, I just keep moving along in some way. The feeling of movement, progress, and personal growth is necessary for our sanity.

I don't see how anyone can be happy with the ordinary dullness of life without activity that is helping make better use of whatever ability he or she may have.

I like the adventure of change and improvement in myself. I want to grow in every possible way. A couch potato, I could never be! Planning, dreaming, and goal setting is important in everyone's life. The action you create will take you to a new adventure in your life. What can be more fun?

It's worth repeating, the more you write, the more it becomes important, the more important it becomes, the more you write. It has a whirlpool effect that will pull you into what you want to do with your life. Nutritionists say, you become what you eat. You also become what you think, so look for a new interest. Be flexible, take a chance, risk a little, and get out of that old rut you are in.

CHAPTER 7

QUOTATIONS

CONFIDENCE.

Develop confidence by writing down what confidence means to you. Write your opinions, they will lead you, at least to what you believe today. Your opinions will change each day, week, or month. So, each time you think of the word, give your thought the respect it deserves with paper and pencil.

I'd like to assure you, you will get a kick out of seeing changes in your thinking You will see it is nothing but personal growth you are going through. It is self-education at it's best, all designed by no one but you. Do some research on your own; it's easy to find out what other people have thought or think about confidence. As you focus on this work you will be surprised with your own depth and the quantity of your ideas. Knowledge and wisdom grows wherever you happen to spend your time. You become what you think about. The following quotes should be just a small beginning; they will give you some ideas. Your own confidence will not be something I gave you. You will find your own and you will enjoy the discovery.

Richard V. Eastman

Whether you think you can or think you can't-you are right.
Henry Ford.

In the moment that you carry this conviction...in that moment your dream will become a reality.
Robert Collier

Nothing in the world can take the place of persistence. Talent will not; nothing is more common than unsuccessful men with talent. Genius will not. Un-rewarded genius is almost a proverb. Education will not; the world is full of educated derelicts. Persistence and determination alone are omnipotent.
Calvin Coolidge.

The strongest single factor in prosperity consciousness is self-esteem: believing you can do it, believing you deserve it, believing you will get it.
Jerry Gillies

Remember the old saying, "Faint heart ne'er won fair lady."
Cervantes.

I admire great men of all classes, those who stand for facts, and for thoughts. I applaud a sufficient man, an officer equal to his office; captains, minister, senators. I like a master standing firm on legs of iron, well-born, rich, handsome, eloquent, loaded with advantages, drawing all men by fascination into tributaries and supporters of his power. Sword and staff, or talents sword-like or staff-like, carry on the work of the world. But I find him greater, when he can abolish himself, and all heroes, by letting in this element of reason, irrespective of persons.
Emerson "Representative Men p. 18"

Building the confidence of followers so that they can achieve their own goals through their own efforts is the responsibility of leadership.

John W. Gardner
On Leadership p. 22

The superior man is always candid and at ease with himself or others; the inferior man is always worried about something.

Confucius

Those who have knowledge are more confident that those who have no knowledge, and they are more confident after they have learned than before.

Plato

The mind is the limit. As long as the mind can envision the fact that you can do something, you can do it as long as you really believe 100 percent.

Arnold Schwarzenegger

I learned this at least, by my experiment; that if one advances confidently in the direction of his dreams, and endeavors to live the life which he has imagined, he will meet with a success unexpected in common hours.

Thoreau

He who believes is strong; he who doubts is weak. Strong convictions precede great actions.

J. F. Clarke

The people who get on in this world are the people who get up and look for the circumstances they want, and, if they can't find them make them.

George Bernard Shaw.

I found that I could find the energy that I could find the determination to keep on going. I learned that your mind can amaze your body, if you just keep telling yourself, I can do it, I can do it, I can do it.

Jon Erickson

Confidence is where you find it, so keep looking, don't ever give up. The following is a direction: Writing is a healthful release for feeling and tensions, a place to advise yourself, clarify goals, and make decisions, a way to nourish yourself with friendship and self-acceptance, a non threatening place to work out relationships with others and to develop your capacity for intimacy, a path to self-awareness and self-knowledge, a place to rehearse future behavior, a technique for focusing your energies on what is immediately important, a way to organize and expand your time, a place to find creative solution to problems, a memory aid, a means of achieving self-identity, a way to enjoy and profit from solitude, a guide to finding clarity in the midst of midst of crisis or change, a device for discovering your path and taking responsibility for the direction of your life.

Tristine Rainer "The New Diary."

Where self-confidence and self-esteem seem unattainable, the emerging individual becomes a highly explosive entity. He tries to derive a sense of confidence and worth by embracing some absolute truth and by identifying himself with the spectacular doing of a leader or some collective body-be it a nation, a congregation, a party, or a mass movement.

Eric Hoffer The Ordeal of Change p.9

Among other things, a leader must recognize the needs of followers or constituents, help them see how those needs can be met, and give them confidence that they can accomplish that result through their own efforts.

John W. Gardner On Leadership   p. 184

Sooner or later all leaders find them selves trying to build confidence. This passage by John Galsworthy bespeaks depth of faith and a grand intent to celebrate that faith, but even more it reflects confidence in the long future. "Let us build a church· so great that those who come after us may think us mad to have attempted it."
John W. Gardner On Leadership p. 194

There have always been deaths in every generation since man lived, but a nation cannot exist without confidence in its leader.
Confucius

There is a romantic notion that the best leaders do not thrust themselves forward but are sought out. In reality, almost all young leaders nominate themselves-over and over, if necessary. They win recognition through a series of acts of presumption. As Edwin P. Hollander puts it, they have a sense of assurance in exercising positive influence, a confidence that others will react affirmatively. It requires confidence to take the risks that leaders take, and confidence to handle the hostility that leaders must absorb.
John W. Gardner In Leadership   p.53

Leaders can do much to preserve the necessary level of trust. The first requirement is that they have the capacity to inspire trust in themselves.
John W Gardner p. 17

In order to succeed we must first believe that we can.   Michael Korda.

The only way you can be rich is to be a rich person. A rich person already has the things they want and is only sharing their richness with others. Being human is sharing, revealing, and being vulnerable by having the courage to take a risk with another human. If you avoid making a positive statement wherever you can, then you are not acting with confidence. You have given yourself a loophole for escape in case of need.

If you are beating drums, beat them loudly, if you know the music. If you don't know the music, learning it will give you confidence. Working with confidence, purpose and set goals assures belief that there are answers to all problems. Confidence comes from independently striving and arriving at where you feel you want to be.

R. V.E.

Bonaparte relied on his own sense, and did not care a bean for other people's.

Emerson

Do not wish to be anything but what you are, and try to be that perfectly.

St. Francis De Sales

These, then, are my last words to you: Be not afraid of life. Believe that life is worth living and your belief will help create the fact.

William James

The ultimate test of education is whether it makes people comfortable in the presence of options; which is to say, whether it enables them to pursue their possibilities with confidence.

Norman Cousins   Human Options p. 17

How does a confident person act? One stands tall, one speaks with authority, one stays in control. If you stand tall, speak with authority, and stay in control-in short, if you act like a confident person-then you will become a confident person.

Dr. James E. Loehr/Peter J. McLaughlin
Mentally Tough p. 63

Your environment gives you plenty of reasons to feel negative, and that's the normal response. When you feel that response, you can use the Marine Technique to advance you to your goals. No matter how negative you feel, act positive. Fake it. Fake it with every part of you at your command. It's only an act, but act it as well as you possibly can. You will become what you have pretended to be.
Dr. James E. Loehr/Peter J. McLaughlin
Mentally Tough p.63

If you believe in yourself, well, then there's nothing you can't accomplish. So don't quit. Don't ever quit.
Harvey Mackay
Swim with the Sharks p. 68

The moment the Englishmen learns to reason and lose their strong confidence in themselves, the British Empire will collapse. For no one can go about conquering the world if he has doubts about himself.
Lin Yutang

Intellectual courage or independence of judgment requires a certain childish, naive confidence in oneself, but this self is the only thing that one can cling to, and the moment a student gives up his right of personal judgment, he is in for accepting all the humbugs of life.
Lin Yutang
The Importance of living p. 364

Everyone muffles his soul for fear he shall be deemed one who thinks well of himself, a seeker after power.
Jacques Barzun
The house of Intellect p. 75

"My strength is as the strength of ten/because my heart is pure."
Tennyson

Trust thyself; every heart vibrates to that iron string.
Emerson

A confident person approaches the realization that he no longer needs to fear what experience may hold, but can welcome it freely as a part of his changing and developing self.
Carl R. Rogers
Freedom to Learn p. 281

If a man has any clear thought or knowledge in him, his aid will be to communicate it, and he will direct his energies to this end; so that the ideas he furnishes are everywhere clearly expressed.
Arthur Schopenhauer
The Art of Literature p. 19

What the mind of man can conceive and believe, the mind of man can achieve.
Napoleon Hill

The only thing that stands between a man and what he wants from life is often merely the will to try it and the faith to believe that it is possible.
Richard M. Devos

In Lichtenbergs Miscellaneous Writing I find this sentence quoted: "Modesty should be the virtue of those who possess no other." Goethe has a well-known saying, which offends many people: "It is only knaves who are modest! Everyone whose verse shows him to be a poet should have a high opinion of himself," relying on the proverb that he is a knave who thinks himself one. And Shakespeare, in many of his sonnets, which gave him the only opportunity he had of speaking of himself, declared, with a confidence equal to his ingenuousness, "that what he writes is immortal.

Arthur Schopenhauer.

No education is better than to offer the child lessons in as many different skills as possible, rather than training in any one particular field. However, in another sense, training a child thoroughly in one field also has its great merit: "excelling in one thing gives confidence in others."

Masaru Ibuka

If we live truly, we shall see truly. It is as easy for the strong man to be strong, as it is for the weak to be weak.

Emerson

I must be myself, I cannot break myself any longer for you, or you. If you can love me for what I am, we shall be the happier. If you cannot, I will still seek to deserve that you should. I will not hide my tastes or aversions.

Emerson
Selected Essays p. 160

The gentleman is a man of truth, lord of his own actions, and expressing that lordship in his behavior; not in any manner possessions. Beyond this fact of truth and real force, the word demotes good-nature or benevolence; manhood first, and them gentleness.

Emerson
Selected Essays p. 383

Montaigne talks with shrewdness, knows the world, and books, and himself, and uses the positive degree; never shrieks, or protest or prays: no weakness, no convulsion, no superlative; does not wish to jump out of his skin, or play any antics, or annihilate space

or time; but is stout and solid; tastes every moment of the day; likes pain, because it makes him feel himself, and realize things; as we pinch ourselves to know that we are awake. He keeps the plain; he rarely mounts or sinks; likes to feel solid ground, and the stones underneath. His writing has no enthusiasms, no aspiration; contented, self respecting, and keeping the middle of the road. There is but one exception-in his love for Socrates. In speaking of him, for once his cheek flushes, and his style rises to passion.
Emerson

Passion holds up the bottom of the world, while genius paints its roof. For unless we have passion, we have nothing to start out in life with at all. It is passion that is the soul of life, the light in the stars, the lilt in music and song, the joy in flowers, the plumage in birds, the charm in woman, and the life in scholarship. It is as impossible to speak of a soul without passion as to speak of music without expression. It is that which gives us inward warmth and the rich vitality which enables us to face life cheerily.
Lin Yutang
The Importance of Living p.9

Living by the "seat of your pants" is the best way, but not without intuition, which comes from experience.
Richard Bandler and John Grinder
from   Frogs into Princes p. 9

A child is confident. He has not learned all of the reason why a thing cannot be done. He ignores obstacles because he does not know they exist. This we learn from the child. The more childlike we are in our approach to problems, the more creative we will be. Try the fresh approach of a child.
Wilfred A. Peterson
Adventures in The Art of Living p. 37

He can who thinks he, can.
Orison Swett Marden

An Origin is a person who feels that he is director of his life. He feels that what he is doing is the result of his own free choice; he is doing it because he wants to do it, and the consequences of his activity will be valuable to him. He thinks carefully about what he wants in this world, now and in the future, and chooses the most important goals ruling out those that are for him too easy or too risky... he is genuinely self-confident because he has determined how to reach his goals through his own efforts... he is aware of his abilities and limitations. In short, an Origin is master of his fate. A Pawn is a person who feels that someone, or something else, is in control of his fate. He feels that others have imposed what he is doing on him. He is doing it because he is forced to, and the consequences of his activity will not be a source of pride to him. Since he feels that external factors determine his fate, the Pawn does not consider carefully his goals in life, nor does he concern himself about what he himself can do to further his cause. Rather he hopes for a Lady Luck to smile on him.

David A. Kolb/Irwin M. Rubin/James
McIntyre p. 419 Organizational Psychology.

It was her own inner strength that made Indira Gandhi a major and controversial figure for over two decades.

John W. Gardner
On Leadership p. 44

Nothing is easier than to turn cynical; nothing is more essential than to avoid it. For the ultimate penalty of cynicism is not that the individual will come to distrust others but that he will come to distrust himself. It is not necessary, in order to avoid cynicism, to believe blindly that human beings are always good. We are required not to invent good human beings but to help give them faith in themselves and to help keep them going.

Human Options by Norman Cousins p. 48

No person can be truly at peace with himself if he does not live up to his moral capacity.
Norman Cousins
Human Options p. 45

Lets us think about ourselves. If our purposes are frail, if the value we attach to the idea of progress is small, if our concern for the next generation is uninspired, then we can bow low before the difficulty, stay as we are, and accept the consequences of drift. But if we have some feeling for the gift of life and the uniqueness of life, if we have confidence in freedom, growth, and the miracle of vital change, then difficulty loses its power to intimidate.
Norman Cousins
Human Options. p. 51

The most magnificent cathedrals are not outside you but inside you.
Albert Schweitzer.

A master of him-self is stronger than a conqueror of a city.
Proverbs 16:32

Every one who really thinks for himself is so far like a monarch. His position is undelegated and supreme. His judgments, like royal decrees, spring from his own sovereign power and proceed directly from himself. He acknowledges authority as little as a monarch admits a command; he subscribes to nothing but what he has himself authorized.
Arthur Schopenhauer
The Art of Literature.

There is a kind of elevation, which does not depend on fortune; it is a certain air, which distinguishes us, and seems to destine us for great things; it is a price, which we imperceptibly set upon ourselves.
Francois De La Rochefoucauld

COURAGE

The way you act says more than what your words express. Do you have self-respect and respect for others? How does your home look, and what does your personal appearance and dress express? Do you spend your time well; do you waste or become fanatical about its use? Is there flexibility where it appears sensible? Do you make human and eye contact with ease? Are you too formal, to rigid, too aloof, or too cool? Are you too loose, too friendly, too eager to please, too much of a buddy?

Do you appear emotionally healthy? Are you more or less of normal weight? Are you generally comfortable, and specifically in your body? Are you preoccupied or present; do you appear to be looking past or beyond people? Do you convey an air of inner peace or are you jumpy and fidgety? Do you smoke? It is usually a sign of much anxiety. Do you talk to much or to little? Depending on your age or sex, are you comfortable as you are with your position in life. Does your behavior and manner say that you are proud of your sexual orientation? Are you too friendly or hostile with the opposite Sex? A male chauvinist or women's liberationist is often driven by their own agenda.

Reuben Bar-Levav. M.D.

Never has a man who has bent himself been able to make others stand straight.

Mencius.

The whole wide world
is but a narrow bridge-
And one's main task
Is not to fear at all.

Rabbi Nachman Bratzlav
1772-1811

Thomas A. Edison was far and away the calmest man I have ever known. He had no frustration complexes. He had no fears.

107

He had no regrets about anything or anyone. He had no grandiose ideas of his own importance, but he did have humility of the heart, which made him truly great. Mr. Edison knew no such reality as "failure" because he had discovered the supreme secret, which leads to pace of mind and understanding of the source and power of the mind. Without the aid of that supreme secret, Mr. Edison never would have become the world's number one inventor. The majority of men quit trying when overtaken one time by defeat.

Napoleon Hill.

To base the reward for virtuous actions on other men's approval is to rely on too uncertain and shaky a foundation. Especially in so corrupt and ignorant an age as this, the good opinion of the crowd is injurious. Whom are you trusting to see what is praiseworthy? God preserve me from being an honest man according to the criterion that I daily see every man apply himself, to his own advantage! What ere once vices have now become customs.

Montaigne
Selected Essays p. 238

Nothing is at lasting sacred but the integrity of your own mind. Let a man then know his worth, and keep things under his feet. Let him not peep or steal, to skulk up and down with the air of a charity-boy, a bastard, or an interloper in the world, which exists for him. Have no regrets. Never imitate. Nothing can bring you peace but yourself.

Ralph Waldo Emerson
Selected Essays P. XXIII.

Who so would be a man, must be a nonconformist.
Emerson

Courage can take us into a world that we did not think possible. It can make us understand our own strengths; some that have long been hidden, some we are not yet aware of.   It's important I think that we look into ourselves for abilities and talent that need the seed of courage. It seems, so often we are not aware of our own potential. We need courage to make mistakes and learn from our mistakes. Too often, we remain in our own private little rut or hut, without venturing into the real world where losing is easily possible; where it is necessary that we pick ourselves up after failing or being knocked down by our circumstances. I like the philosophy of living where life is fun, scary, or intellectually interesting a learning situation.

We need to test ourselves in every way possible. Safe and sane has very few rewards. This kind of attitude requires that we live within the boundary of our conscience. We must have good manners; respect for other people and their property. We must provide a service to others and the world we live in. We all want to feel good about ourselves. Most of us, it seems, want to be someone's hero at some time in our life. It's just the way we are. Courage opens the door for honesty and integrity.

Through daily choice and practice:
    by mothering
    she became a mother,
  by cooking a cook,
  by writing a writer,
    by traveling a traveler,
The habit of courage
      permitted her to see and
    feel and live life.
                Unknown

Apathy adds up, in the long run, to cowardice.
Courage is nothing but knowledge; it makes us more alive, beyond comparison, better, braver and more industrious.
                Emerson

Richard V. Eastman

Liberty is the secret of happiness, and courage is the secret of liberty. I will despise myself later if I look back on my life and realize that I had the talent and the ability to do great things but could not find the courage to try.

To claim our dignity and to find our courage, we need anxiety to help us. Dignity is the courage to be yourself. Courage is acting with fear, not without it. Courage is a three-letter work-and that word is yes.

Walter Anderson
Courage is a Three-Letter word.

Our challenge is to live with anxiety, to remind ourselves that it is an asset to our well-being. It can be our ally.

Walter Anderson
Courage is a Three Letter Word.

The braver man is not he who feels no fear, for that were stupid and irrational; but he, whose noble soul is fear subdued, and bravely dares the danger nature shrinks from.

Joanna Baille

The only limit to our realization of tomorrow will be our doubts of today.

Franklin D. Roosevelt

The barrier between, success is not something which exists in the real word; it is composed purely and simply of doubts about ability.

Mark Caine.

These, then, are my last words to you: be not afraid of life. Believe that life is worth living and your belief will help create the fact.

William James

The scars you acquire by exercising courage will never make you feel inferior.

D.A. Battista

Success is never final, and failure is never fatal; its courage that counts. All of the significant battles are waged within the self.

Sheldon Kopp.

This is the test of your manhood: How much is there left in you after you have lost everything outside of yourself!

Orison Sweet Marden

Comedian/Director Woody Allen once commented that while one could inherit wealth, looks, status and perhaps intellect, one could not inherit courage. Courage one earns by one's life actions and a noble virtue. Everyone wants to be proud, and we need to find the things that make us proud.

Walter Anderson

Courage is a Three Letter Word.

You gain strength, courage and confidence by every experience which you must stop and look fear in the face. You must do the thing you think you cannot do.

Eleanor Roosevelt.

Dignity is the courage to be yourself.

Walter Anderson Courage is a Three Letter Word.

You have a remarkable ability, which you never acknowledged before. It is to look at a situation and know whether you can do it. And I mean really know the answer.

Carl Frederick.

We can do only what we think we can do. We can be only what we think we can be. We can have only what we think we can have. What we do, what we are, what we have, all depend upon what we think.

Robert Collier

The strongest single factor in prosperity consciousness is self-esteem; believing you can do it, believing you deserve it, believing you will get it.

Jerry Gillies

The difference between a successful person and others is not a lack of strength, not a lack of knowledge, but rather in a lack of will.

Vincent T. Lombardi

Success is never final, and failure is never fatal, its courage that counts. Courage is resistance to fear, mastery of fear-not absence of fear.

Mark Twain

I do not think there is any other quality so essential to success of any kind as the quality of perseverance. It overcomes almost everything, even nature.

John D. Rockerfeller.

Opportunity rarely knocks on your door. Knock rather on opportunity's door in which you ardently wish to enter.

B.C. Forbes.

Accept the challenges, so that you may feel the exhilaration of victory.

General George S. Patton

Our greatest glory is not in never failing, but in rising every time we fall.
Confucius

Adversity reveals genius, prosperity conceals it.
Horace.

History has demonstrated that the most notable winners usually encountered heartbreaking obstacles before they triumphed. They won because they refused to become discouraged by their defeats.
B.C. Forbes

Opportunity often comes disguised in the form of misfortune, or temporary defeat.
Napoleon Hill

In the middle of difficulty lies opportunity.
Albert Einstein

You can summon courage, once you understand what courage really is.
Walter Anderson
Courage is a Three Letter Word.

Courage and intelligence are the best qualities worth cultivation.
Samuel Johnson

Courage requires that you become a part of the solution rather than a part of the problem. You are remembered for the rules you break.
Douglas Mac Arthur.

Who is the most cowardly person you know? After looking around, you can see; it is usually the person who is trying to please everyone and is uneasy if even a single person disapproves of their action.

For I am nothing.....if not critical.
  Shakespeare.

Passion gives successful people the energy and courage to get out of line, to be different, which in turn gives them a shot at true excellence.

Those who seek to be different grow used to being stared at. Society is fascinated by those who are not fascinated by it. Courage is not absence of despair; it is, rather, the capacity to move ahead in spite of despair. If you do not express your own original ideas, if you do not listen to your own being, you will have betrayed yourself. Everyone should develop fully his or her potential abilities and grow courageous in thought and straight forward in character.
  Masaru Ibuka
  Kindergarten is Too Late p. 181

Nothing splendid has ever been achieved except by those who dared believe that something inside of them was superior to circumstance.
  Bruce Barton

Courage is the capacity to confront what can be imagined.
  Leo Rosten.

Courage is a result of reasoning. A brave mind is always impregnable.
  Waiter Irving.

Stone walls do not a prison make, nor iron bars a cage.
Richard Lovelace.

A man is literally what he thinks
James Allen

The barrier between, success is not something which exists in
the real world; it is composed purely and simply of doubts about
ability.
Mark Caine.

Courage is nothing but knowledge.
Emerson

Genuine growth means having the courage and confidence to
try new things, and in the process, to let go of old ones.

Lincoln openly admitted his doubts as you and I have ours,
but had the courage to move ahead in spite of these doubts.

The credit belongs to the man who is actually in the arena,
who's face is marred by dust and sweat and blood; who strives
valiantly; who errs and comes short again and again, who knows
the great enthusiasms, the great devotions, and spends himself
in a worthy cause; who at the best, knows the triumph of high
achievement; and who at the worst, if he fails, at least fails while
daring greatly, so that his place shall never be with those cold and
timid souls who know neither victory nor defeat.
Theodore Roosevelt

Give me the young man who has brains enough to make a fool
of himself.
Stevenson

I no longer think a project is worthwhile unless it scare me half to death. You must move ahead in spite of the fear, which is courage defined.

Deanie Francis Mills.

Do not follow where the path my lead. Go instead where there is no path and leave a trail. Always bear in mind that your own resolution to succeed is more important than any other one thing.

Abraham Lincoln

All our dreams can come true-if we have the courage to pursue them.

Walt Disney

He who has not fully tried his strength leaves you to guess if he has any power left, and if he has been tested to his utmost. He who sinks under his burden, betrays his measure and the weakness of his shoulders.

Montaigne

Men to often have not the courage to correct because they have not the courage to suffer correction. Socrates always welcomed with a smile the contradictions offered to his arguments. This was due to his strength, the advantage was certain to fall to his side, he accepted them as occasions for fresh triumphs.

Montaigne

All things are difficult before they are easy.
John Norley

The people who get on in this world are the people who get up and look for the circumstances they want, and, if they can't find them, make them.

George Bernard Shaw

Nothing in the world can take the place of persistence. Talent will not; nothing is more common than unsuccessful men with talent. Genius will not; unrewarded genius is almost a proverb. Education will not; the world is full of educated derelicts. Persistence and determination alone are omnipotent.

Calvin Coolidge.

There's no thrill in easy sailing when the skies are clear and blue, there's no joy in merely doing things which any one can do But, there is some satisfaction what is mighty sweet to take, when you reach a destination that you thought you'd never make.

Spirerra

Things may come to those who wait, but only the things left by those who hustle.

Abraham Lincoln.

The feeling of individual helplessness is a great and growing problem. But there is an answer. It is not very complicated. Each person has inside him a basic decency and goodness. If he listens to it and acts on it, he is giving a great deal of what it is the world most needs. But, it takes courage.

Albert Schweitzer

There is a certain blend of courage, integrity, character and principle, which has no satisfactory dictionary name but has been called different things at different time in different countries. Our American name for it is "guts."

Louis Adamic
A Study in Courage 1944

Live each day as if your life had just begun.
Goethe

He who loses wealth loosed much; he who loses a friend loses more; but he that loses courage loses all.
Cervantes

Courage is doing what you're afraid to do. There can be no courage unless you're scared.
Eddie Rickenbacker

The only thing that stands between a man and what he wants from life is often merely the will to try it and the faith to believe that it is possible.
Richard M. Devos

In the middle of difficulty lies opportunity.
Albert Einstein

If I were asked to give what I consider the single most useful bit of advice for all humanity it would be this: Expect trouble as an inevitable part of life and when it comes, hold your head high, look it squarely in the eye and say, "I will be bigger then you. You cannot defeat me."
Ann Landers

Obstacles will look large or small to you according to whether you re large or small.
Orison Sweet Marden

What the superior man seeks is in himself: what the small man seeks is in others.
Francois La Rochefoucauld

Courage is resistance to fear, mastery of fear-not absence of fear.
Mark Twain

Nothing splendid has ever been achieved except by those who dared believe that something inside of them was superior to circumstance.
Bruce Barton

Courage is the capacity to confront what can be imagined.
Leo Rosten

Courage is a result of reasoning . A brave mind is always impregnable.
Jeremy Collier

Little minds attain and are subdued by misfortunes; but great minds rise above them.
Washington Irving.

We may affirm absolutely that nothing great in the world has been accomplished without passion.
George Wilhelm Friedrich Hegel

If I were to give what I consider the single most useful bit of advice for all humanity it would be this: Expect trouble as an inevitable part of life.
Ann Landers.

Courage is a special kind of knowledge; the knowledge of how to fear what ought to be feared, and how not to fear what ought not to be feared. From this knowledge comes an inner strength that subconsciously inspires us to push on in the face of great difficulty.. What can seem impossible is often possible, with courage.
Wynn Davis
The Best of Success.

One man with courage is a majority.
Andrew Jackson

If you would not be forgotten as soon as you are gone, either write things worth reading or do things worth writing
Benjamin Franklin.

It is my hope of education-every infant to develop fully his potential abilities and to grow up courageous in thought and straightforward in character.
Masaru Ibuka

Courage is like love; it must have hope for nourishment.
Napoleon Bonaparte.

Every man of courage is a man of his word.
Pierre Corneille.

Like love, courage is no joking matter. If it yields once, it will have to yield again, and again. The same difficulty will have to be conquered later on, and it would have been better to get it over with.
Baltasar Gracian.

It takes vision and courage to create--it takes faith and courage to prove.
Owen D. Young.

Pay no attention to what the critics say; there has never been a statue erected to a critic.
Jean Sibelius.

Courage is the first of human qualities because it is the quality which guarantees all the others.
Winston Churchill

You might as well fall flat on your face as lean over too far backward.

James Thurber.

Conscience is the root of all true courage; if a man would be brave let him obey his conscience.

James Freeman Clarke.

CHAPTER 8

QUOTATIONS

CREATIVITY

Very few people do anything creative after the age of thirty-five. The reason is that very few people do anything creative before the age of thirty-five.

Joel Hildebrand.

Dr. Johnson said, "I speak to be instructed." He said, "My Lord, my Lord, I do not desire all this ceremony let us tell our minds to one another quietly." After the debate was over, he said, "I have got lights on the subject today, which I had not before."

Samuel Johnson

Encourage Problem Solving
Kid: My teacher hates me.
Dad: What are you going to do about it?
Kid: I'm not going back to school.
Dad: That's one solution. What's another?
Kid: Maybe you should talk to the teacher, Dad.
Dad: That's one solution. What's another?
Kid: Figure out how to please the teacher.

Richard V. Eastman

Dad: that's one solution. What's another?

Kid: Get a new dad.

Landis has a house rule: If a child has a problem, he must come up with at least three solutions. Instead of teaching facts, it's important to teach possibility," he said. "I taught my children that life is an experiment. The key with kids is making them comfortable with uncertainty. When people find answers, they stop looking."

Orange County Register
Thursday Oct. 26, 1989 p. J4

We must use creativity to the hilt and encourage others to do the same.

Camus

Creativity can and should be your life. It is an opportunity for you to blossom in every way that you will eventually live. Thinking should be your most important goal in life.

Tristine Rainer
The New Diary

Blake thought that creative power should be kept alive in all people for all of their lives. And so do I. Why? Because it is life itself. It is the Spirit. In fact it is the only important thing about us. The rest of us is legs and stomach, materialistic cravings and fears. How could we keep it alive? By using it, by letting it out, by giving some time to it.

Brenda Ueland
If You Want to Write.

I am for amateurism in all fields. I love amateur philosophers, amateur poets, amateur photographers, amateur magicians, amateur botanists and amateur aviators.

Lin Yutang
The Importance of living

There is one thing stronger than all the armies in the world, and that is an idea whose time has come.
Victor Hugo

Happiness lies in the joy of achievement and the thrill of creative effort.
Franklin D Roosevelt

Remember, you cannot do what you cannot imagine. But, you can imagine anything. The source and center of all man's creative power is his power of making images, or the power of imagination.
Robert Collier

First comes thought, then organization of that thought into ideas and plans; then transformation of those plans into reality. The beginning, as you will observe is in your imagination.
Napoleon Hill

Psychologists say that creativity flourishes in children whose parents make it a priority. Nurturing creativity doesn't require expensive private lessons. It's a matter of attitude at home. "You want to keep alive the children's passion, their intrinsic motivation, their joy of doing things for the sake of doing them.
Teresa Amabile
Growing Up Creative

If children know their parents appreciate creative and original things, they'll be more likely to be creative.
Mark Runco Director of Research Center for Creativity, Cal. State University. Fullerton

Anais Nin celebrated creativity as a way of life. She advocated a concept of the creative person not as an alienated "artist" but as an alive, curious individual who is ever finding new ways to grow, expand, and enjoy the moment. She used the diary not to escape from life but to live it more fully and deeply.

Tristine Rainer

Creativity and therapy become one and the same in the New Diary-an active communication with self. Each compliments the other, and arises out of the other. Creativity, like self-awareness, depends upon being in touch with your intellectual and emotional processes, upon listening for, valuing, and cultivating what come from within. As a diarist you are immersed in the habit of genuine self-communication, so that creativity becomes part of your daily life. Once your creative spirit has been freed and nurtured in the journal you are likely to discover an added benefit of the diary as a source book for creative projects.

Tristine Rainer
The New Diary

As a protected place in which to refresh your spirit, keeping a diary can be an important aid for the professional writer. It also serves the writer as a place to "work out" regularly. Anais Nin recommended in. The Novel of The Future, writing as one practices the piano every day keeps one nimble, and then when the great moments of inspiration come, one is in good form, supple and smooth.

Tristine Rainer
The New Diary

Whether you use the New Diary as a scrapbook for creative ideas, as a record of the details of a business meeting, as a road map of your emotional life, or as part of your personal spiritual search is your choice. At one time you may rely on it to solve problems, at another time to discover new pleasures in the context of your life.

We often write what we feel needs to be written. The diary is a never-ending process of search and discovery. It changes as you change; and by acting as a mirror to the self it encourages personal transformation. What I have called the new diary will continue to evolve, change, and re-create itself. For the diary, so intimately linked to time, is ever renewed and cannot be outdated. The diary has always recorded the present as a gesture of faith in the future. I want to be a better man tomorrow because of today's activity.

Tristine Rainer
The New Diary

All inspirations seem at the moment of conception to be genuine, but it takes time to tell which will be fertile. In the diary the collected inspirations for a book, poem, painting, film, sculpture, musical composition, or any other creative work lie side by side in incubation. Some seem to augment their meaning in relationship to others; some seem to drop away as irrelevant; some merged into large, more comprehensive ideas.

Tristine Rainer
The New Diary
Trust only movement.
Alfred Adler.

Every noble work is at first impossible.
Thomas Carlyle.

Every person has some splendid traits and if we confine our contacts so as to bring those traits into action, there is no need of ever being bored or irritated or indignant.
Gelett Burgess.

Congratulate yourselves if you have done something strange and extravagant and broken the monotony of a decorous (Politically correct.)age.
Ralph Waldo Emerson.

Man is made to create, from the poet to the potter.
Benjamin Disraeli.

Early in life I had to choose between honest arrogance and hypocritical humility. I chose honest arrogance and have seen no occasion to change.
Frank Lloyd Wright.

Man ought always to have something that he prefers to life; otherwise life itself will seem to him tiresome and void.
Johaann Gottfried Seume

There are glimpses of heaven to us in every act, or thought, or word that raises us above ourselves.
Arthur Penrhyn Stanley.

They build too low who build beneath the skies.
Edward Young.

The measure of the creator is the amount of life he puts into his work.
Carl Van Doren.

The art of a people is a true mirror of their minds.
Jawaharlel Nehru

EDUCATION

The great men and women of our time, those who have their name in history books, had no college degree. They found and designed their own education. Their learning was the result of focus on whatever they had a natural interest in. Many wrote mini-essays on a clear and specific one-word subject. They knew if they could clearly focus on their gut feelings, they're true feelings; the light in the end of their tunnel; the light of their life would shine brighter. They followed their own thinking, made their own decisions.
R V.E.

If there is an urgent need for the well-being of our children, it is that they feel good about themselves. They must feel "literate." They must feel as capable as anyone, when it comes to learning and understanding our language. If they don't understand, they must think they soon will. There is no doubt they realize the need to work, and that they must keep trying.

Children by their very nature, love to learn, so "working at it," is something they do naturally. I think demanding language perfection before they are ready is causing a double-bind situation. They can't write because they don't understand the language. They don't understand the language, so they can't write. The demand for perfectionism, without the timing being correct destroys their ability to function.

Few, if any people can continue to function when they are making a fool-of-themselves. The solution is to allow them to function at their own pace, some part of each day. The freedom to work at there own pace will allow learning without "unnecessary" frustration. Success will multiply enthusiasm for work Success breeds success.

Timing is important. My experience with timing tells me that it is important in all things: Love, marriage, business, humor, etc.. All battles in life are won with timing that fits the need. History has proven the genius of perfect timing is often the difference between success and failure. Excellence has a time and place, depending almost entirely upon each individual's readiness to seize the moment. Desire must be there and skills must be ready for the opportunity-what ever it happens to be.

The rules of grammar are the biggest problem our children have. They are suffering because they have not paid their dues. Adult's, who don't realize students are not ready, throw perfection upon them. The demands are too much for the skills they have. They need more practice, more volume, more experience with the use of words. The frustration they feel is forced on them by grades and adult criticism.

Richard V. Eastman

FINDING YOUR PASSION

What you do must be consistent with who you are and what you really want. Stop and think for a few minutes. Answer these questions:

Where do I want to be in five years?
If I were told that I had six months to live,
how would I spend those six months?
What would I want to get done?
Am I deriving any satisfaction out of what I'm
doing now?
Am I living life now, or merely preparing or life?
If they didn't pay me to do what I do, would I still
do it?
If I won a million dollars in the lottery tomorrow,
how would I live? What would I do each day?
If I were to write my own obituary right now,
what would be my most significant
accomplishment?
Is that enough? What would I really like to do?

The answers to those questions will tell you what you need to know about yourself-your true motivations, your passions, the things you love to do. In a word, your goals.

Dr. James E. Loehr and
Peter McLaughlin
"Mentally tough"

When students perceive that they are free to follow their own goals, most of them invest more of themselves in their effort, work harder, and retain and use more of what they have learned, than in conventional courses.

Carl R. Rogers

Adults who think that children must be manipulated for their own good have developed the attitude of a controlling parent who lacks faith in himself the child or humanity or himself.

Carl R. Rogers

We must view young people not as empty bottles to be filled, but as candles to be lit.

Robert H. Shaffer

Adults who think that children must be manipulated for their own good have developed the attitude of a controlling parent who lacks faith in himself, the child, or humanity.

Carl R. Rogers

If I distrust the human being then I must cram him with information of my own choosing, lest he go his own mistaken way. But if I trust the capacity of the human individual for developing his own potentiality, then I can provide him with opportunities and permit him to choose his own direction in his learning.

Carl R. Rogers

I will perhaps be different tomorrow, if I learn something new which changes me.

Montaigne

Whence it happens that, because we have failed to choose their road well, we often spend a lot of time and effort for nothing, trying to train children for things in which they cannot get a foothold.

Montaigne

The authority of those who teach is often an obstacle to whose who want to learn.

Cicero

Teachers get in the way of the students who are trying to reach the goal, set by the teachers! No one-not your parents, nor your teacher, nor your peers can teach you, how to be yourself.
Warren Bennis

One of the reasons mature people stop learning is that they become less and less willing to risk failure.
John W. Gardner.

Josh Billings said, "It is not only the most difficult thing to know oneself, but the most inconvenient one, too." Human beings have always employed an enormous variety of clever devices for running away from our-selves, and the modern world is particularly rich in such stratagems. We can keep ourselves busy, fill our lives with so many diversions, stuff our heads with so much knowledge, involve ourselves with so many people and cover so much ground that we never have time to probe the fearful and wonderful world within. More often than not, we don't want to know ourselves, don't want to live with ourselves.

By middle life most of us are accomplished fugitives from ourselves.
John W Gardner

Education becomes the release of human possibilities and life long growth.
John W.Gardner

Students who are in real contact with problems which are relevant to them, wish to learn, want to grow, seek to discover, endeavor to master, desire to create, move toward self-discipline.
Carl R. Rogers

The only man who is educated is the man who has learned how to learn; the man who has learned how to adapt and change; the man who has realized that no knowledge is secure, that only the process of seeking knowledge gives a basis for security. Changingness, a reliance on process rather than upon static knowledge, is the only thing that makes any sense a goal for education in the modern world.

Carl R. Rogers

We pay a heavy price for our fear of failure. It is a powerful obstacle to growth. It assumes the progressive rearranging of the personality and prevents exploration and experimentation. There is no learning without some difficulty and fumbling. If you want to keep on learning, you must keep on risking failure-all of your life. I am, vividly reminded of Goethe's saying that men will always be making mistakes as long as they are striving for something.

John W Gardner

I believe that we can almost guarantee that meaningful learning will be at an absolute minimum when we prescribe what and when subjects should be learned. If we have similar assignment, standard test, and instructor chosen grades significant learning is improbable, if not impossible.

Carl R. Rogers

There are practical ways of dealing with students, which stimulate and facilitate significant and self-reliant learning. These ways eliminate every one of the elements of conventional education. They do not rely on a carefully prescribed curriculum, but rather on one that is largely self-chosen; instead of standard assignments for all, each student sets his own assignment; lectures constitute the most infrequent mode of instruction, standardized tests lose their sanctified place, grades are either self-determined or become a relatively unimportant index of learning.

Carl R. Rogers

The development of abilities is at least in part a dialogue between the individual and his environment. If he has it to give and the environment demands it, the ability will develop. Most of us have potentialities that have not been developed simply because the circumstances of our lives never called them forth.

Exploration of the full range of his own potentialities is not something that the self-renewing man leaves to the chances of life. It is something he purses systematically to the end of his days. And by potentialities I mean not just skills, but the full range of his capacities for sensing, wondering, learning, understanding, loving and aspiring.

The ultimate goal of the educational system is to shift to the individual the burden of pursuing his own education.

This means doing away with the gross inequalities of opportunity imposed on some of our citizens by race prejudice and economic hardship. And it means a continuous and effective operation of "talent salvage" to assist young people to achieve the promise that is in them.

John W.Gardner

It is in fact nothing short of a miracle that the modern methods of instruction have not yet entirely strangled the holy curiosity of inquiry; for the delicate little planet, aside form stimulation, stands mainly in need of freedom; without this it goes to wrack and ruin without fail

Albert Einstein

If you tell children often enough that they are Clumsy, Ugly, Stupid, or Incapable, they will in time become just that. At some level, the mind accepts and retains repeated statements and beliefs as the truth, even thought they may be far from it.

Benjamin Hoff

One day well spent is to be preferred to an eternity of error.
Cicero

We learn how to make decisions by making decisions.
Ancient proverb

I find that a great part of the information I have; was acquired by looking up something and finding something else on the way.
Eugene E. Wilson.

Some will never learn anything because they understand everything too soon.
Thomas Blount.

If, as is our custom, the teacher undertakes to regulate many minds of such different capacities and forms with the same lesson and a similar amount of guidance, it is no wonder if in a whole race of children they find barely two of three who reap any proper fruit from their instruction. (This was written before 1592; and we still have that problem today, 400 years later.)
Montaigne

Carl Rogers asks the question; will learning move outside of the "halls of learning," leaving them for only those who want to conform?

The aim of good teaching is to the turn the young learner, by nature a little copycat, into an independent, self-propelling creature, who cannot merely learn but study- that is work as his own boss to the limit of his powers. This is to turn pupils into students, and it can be done on any rung of the ladder of learning.
Jacques Barzun

The humble knowledge of thy-self is surer way to God than the deepest search after science.
Thomas A. Kempis

Education is freedom.
Andre Gide.

It seems to me that anything that can be taught to another is relatively inconsequential and has little or no significant influence on behavior. Ones' own thinking makes a difference.
Carl Rogers

We know what we are, but know not what we may be.
Shakespeare

Vitally important for a young man or woman is first to realize the value of education, and then to cultivate earnestly, aggressively, ceaselessly; the habit of self-education. Without fresh supplies of knowledge, the brain will not develop healthily and vigorously any more than the body can be sustained without fresh supplies of food.
B.C. Forbes.

It is the privilege to learn to use his own mind rather than somebody else's mind.
Howard Lowry

The ultimate goal of the educational system is to shift to the individual the burden of pursuing: his own education.
John Gardner

Our educational system seems to have developed a community of faith and obedience. It should be replaced with knowledge and the will to make a difference.
H.G. Wells

They know enough who know how to learn.
Henry Adams

The foundation of every state is the education of its youth.
Diogenes

Children are naturally fascinated and excited by grown-up words.
John R. Silber

Only the educated are free.
Epictetus

The most manifest sign of wisdom is a continual cheerfulness.
Montaigne

Treat a man as he is and he will remain as he is. Treat a man as he can and should be and he will become as he can and should be.
Goethe

"So much does the soul require an object at which to aim," wrote Montaigne, "that when it does not have one, it will turn it's violence upon itself, and create a false and fantastic problem, in which it does not even believe, rather than not have something to work upon. If you have education-chance and accident have less influence on your life. Education can guide your own destiny. When young people learn what and who they are it helps them to think about what they wish to become as individuals and as a people.
John W Gardner

I agree with Plutarch, the Aristotle did not waste his great pupil's time on lesson in the construction of syllogisms, or on the principles of geometry, but taught him wise precepts on the subject of valour prowess, magnanimity, temperance, and that assurance which knows no fear.
Montaigne

In other words he did not teach rules of logic and deduction, or the principles of geometry, but taught him wise rules on the subject of courage, physical skills, to think "big" about himself and his effect upon the world. He taught him to think on a grand scale, with strength and power of his own design. He taught him that he could make a difference in the world. Personal self-restraint was important to him. He taught him ambition, generosity, forgiveness, liberalism and tolerance. He taught him to be comfortable with himself; to have hope, confidence and belief in himself. Self-respect was important with self assurance that knows no fear.

R. V.E.

Change is so swift that the latest thing today may be old-fashioned by the time young people enter adulthood. So they must be taught in such a way that they can learn for themselves the new things of tomorrow. In all subjects it means teaching habits of mind that will be useful in new situations: curiosity, open-mindness, objectivity, respect for evidence and the capacity to think critically; education for versatility.

John W.Gardner

Almost everybody is a teacher at some time or other during his life.

Jacques Barzun

The founding fathers in their wisdom decided that children are an unnatural strain on parents. So they provided jails called schools, equipped with torture called education.

School is where you go between when your parents can't take you and industry can't take you.

John Updike

The discovery of talent is only one side, perhaps the easier side of self-development. The other side is self-knowledge. The maximum "Know-thyself"-so ancient....so deceptively simple...so difficult to follow...has gained in richness of meaning as we learn more about man's nature.

John W. Gardner

Every man is the architect of his own future.
Appins Claudins Caecus

Resolve to be thyself: And know that he who finds himself, loses his misery.
Matthew Amold

The kingdom of God is within you Luke 17:21

Soap and education are not as sudden as a massacre, but they are more deadly in the long run.
Mark Twain

If you want a thing done well, do it yourself.
Napoleon Bonaparte.

The first forty years of life give us the text; the next thirty supply the commentary.
Arthur Schopenhauer

Stupidity and a confused mind are not to be cured by a word of admonition; and we may fitly say of this kind of correction what Cyrus replied to one who urged him to harangue his army when on the point of entering into battle. "That men are not suddenly made brave and warlike by a fine harangue, any more than a man immediately becomes a musician after hearing a good song" It needs a preliminary apprenticeship, along and continued education.
Montaigne

Cease to ruled by dogmas and authorities; look at the world.
Bacon

The scientific method is this: To make no unnecessary hypotheses, to trust no statements without verification, to test all things as rigorously as possible, to keep no secrets, to attempt no monopolies, to give out ones' best modestly and plainly, serving no other end but knowledge.
Francis Bacon

Most men are old fogies at twenty-five because they have ceased to grow.
William James

A man doesn't learn to understand anything unless he loves it.
Goethe

I find the great thing in this world is not so much where we stand as in what direction we are moving
Oliver Wendell Homes

There is no lock or seal on the knowledge thoughtful reading makes available to us-no abracadabra is necessary to release it. It is free and open to anyone who has the ambition to step up and help themselves.
George H Lorimer.

To know by heart is not to know: it is to retain what we have given our memory to keep. What we know rightly we dispose of, without looking at the model, without turning our eye towards our books. Sad competence. a purely a bookish competence! I intend it to serve as decoration. not as foundation, accord to the opinion of Plato, who says that steadfastness, faith, and sincerity are the real philosophy.
Montaigne

The gain from study is to have become better and wiser by it.
Montaigne

Teachers attempt to control their entire class with the same lessons, even though they all have different levels of interest, talent, and ability. Carl Rogers would say, "I would rather facilitate thinking than tell what the thought should be.
R.V.E.

(Worth Reading) The wrong reason for going to school

We must give up the idea that a man's knowledge can be tested or measured in any form whatsoever. Chuangtse has well said, "Alas, my life is limited, while knowledge is limitless!" The pursuit of knowledge is, after all, only like the exploration of a new continent, or "an adventure of the soul," as Anatole France says, and it will remain a pleasure, instead of becoming a torture, if the spirit of exploration with an open, questioning, curious and adventurous mind is maintained.

Instead of the measured, uniform and passive cramming of information, we have to place this ideal of a positive, growing individual pleasure.

Once the diploma and the marks are abolished. or treated for what they are worth, the pursuit of knowledge becomes positive, for the student is at least forced to ask himself why he studies at all.

At present, the question is already answered for the student, for there is no question in his mind that he studies as a freshman in order to become a sophomore, and studies as a sophomore in order to become junior. All such extraneous considerations should be brushed aside, for the acquisition of knowledge is nobody else's business but one's own.

At present, all students study for the registrar, and many of the good students study for their parents or teacher or their future wives, that they may not seem ungrateful to their parents who are spending so much money for their support at college, or because they wish to appear nice to a teacher who is nice and conscientious to them, or that they may go out of school and earn a higher salary to feed their families. I suggest that all such thoughts are immoral. The pursuit of knowledge should remain nobody else's business but one's own, and only then can education become a pleasure and become positive.

Lin Yutang,

The moment you come to a conclusion as to what intelligence is, you cease to be intelligent. That is what most of the older people have done: they have come to conclusions. Therefore they have ceased to be intelligent. So you have found out one thing right off: that an intelligent mind is an inquiring mind, a mind that is watching, learning, studying.

J. Krishnamurti

Not to imitate but to discover-that is education. is it not? It is very easy to conform to what your society and your parents and teacher tell you. That is a safe and easy way of existing; but that is not living because in it there is fear and decay. To live is to find out for yourself what is true, and you can do this only when there is freedom.

J. Krishnamurti

I find that another way of learning for me is to state my own uncertainties, to try to clarify my puzzlement's, and thus get closer to the meaning that my experience actually seems to have.

Carl R. Rogers

I am always fascinated by the sureness behind statements of college students such as "I am lousy at math," "I cannot draw," or "I am no good at literature." Such statements are usually based on school grades and often do not even reflect a true understanding

of the nature of their intellect. It is possible to find educational opportunities to reexamine almost every aspect of one's abilities.
James L. Adams

No profit grows where is no pleasure taken, in short, study what thou dost affect.
William Shakespeare

Education is a lifelong discipline of the individual by himself, encouraged by a reasonable opportunity to lead a good life.
Jacques Barzun

Education comes form within; it is a man's own doing, or rather it happens to him-sometimes because of the teaching he has had, sometimes in spite of it. No man can say of another; "I educated him" It would be offensive and would suggest that the victim was only a puppy when first taken in hand. But it is a proud thing to say, "I taught him" and a wise one not to specify what.
Jacques Barzun

Education is: "Developing a real capacity for life."
Jacques Barzun

It is only the ignorant who dispise education.
Publius Syrus.

The child will find out about himself if the environment in which he lives helps him to do so. If the parents and teachers are really concerned that the young person should discover what he is, they won't compel him: they will create an environment in which he will come to know himself; If it is important for the child to find out about himself, the attitude should be, "Let us work it out together. " This problem of how to create an environment is which the child can have knowledge of himself is one that concerns everybody-the parent, the teacher, and the children themselves.

Richard V. Eastman

When self-knowledge becomes important: then together we shall create schools of the different kind.
J. Krishnamurti

Seeing much, suffering much, and studying much, are the three pillars of learning.
Benjamin Disraeli.

He who has no inclination to learn more will be very apt to think that he knows enough.
Sir John Powell.

Men learn while they teach.
Seneca

Learning makes a man fit company for himself.
Edward Young.

If a man empties his purse into his head, no man can take it away from him. An investment in knowledge always pays the best interest.
Benjamin Franklin.

The secret of education lies in respecting the pupil.
Ralph Waldo Emerson.

I wish every immigrant could know that Lincoln spent only one year in school under the tutelage of five different teachers, and that the man still could be the author of the Gettysburg address.
John Huston Finley.

The first thing education teaches you is to walk alone.
Alfred Aloysius Horn.

The teach-in represents an attempt to shift education from instruction to discovery, from brainwashing students to brainwashing instructors. It is a big, dramatic reversal.

Herbert Marshall McLuhan.

A degree is not an education, and the confusion on this point is perhaps the gravest weakness in American thinking about education.

Prospect for America.

The best teacher is the one who suggests rather than dogmatizes, and inspires his listener with the wish to teach himself.

Edward Bulwer-Lytton.

Children have to be educated, but they have also to be left to educate themselves.

Ernest Dimnet.

Education is that which remains when one has forgotten everything he learned in school.

Albert Einstein.

Men are born ignorant, not stupid; they are made stupid by education.

Bertrand Russell.

Thank goodness I was never sent to school; it would have rubbed off some of the originality.

Beatrix Potter.

Intelligence is not something that you acquire, like learning; it arises when there is no fear-which means, really, when there is a sense of love. For when there is no fear, there is love.

J. Krishnamurti

To cultivate freedom is the real function of education. Your parents, and your own desires want you to be identified with something or other in order to be happy, secure. But to be intelligent you must break through all the influences that enslave and crush you.

J. Krishnamurti

If you think something is important, really worth while, you give your heart to it and then it will find success, but most of us do not give our hearts to anything. The function of education is to help you from childhood not to imitate anybody, but to be yourself all the time.

J. Krishnamurti

Should not education help you to find out what you really love to do so that from the beginning to the end of your life you are working at something which you feel is worthwhile and which for you has deep significance? Otherwise, for the rest of your days, you will be miserable. Not knowing what you really want to do, your mind falls into a routine in which there is only boredom decay and death.

J. Krishnamurti

In a class room when you stare out of the window or pull somebody's hair, the teacher tells you to pay attention. Which means what? That you are not interested in what you are studying and so the teacher samples you to pay attention, which is not attention at all. Attention comes when you are dearly interested in something, for when you love to find out all about it then your whole mind, your whole being is there.

J. Krishnamurti

Living safely generally means living in imitation and therefore in fear. Surely, the function of education is to help each one of us to live freely without fear, is it not? And to create an atmosphere in which there is no fear requires a great deal of thinking on your part as well as on the part of the teacher, the educator.

J. Krishnamurti

Surely, education has no meaning unless it helps you to understand the vast expanse of life with all its subtleties with its extraordinary beauty, its sorrow and joys.

J. Krishnamurti

Often forgotten by Progressive Education is the thought that all dealing with those taught should to a certain degree be contradictory, by no means all kindness. The customer is always right, perhaps, but not the student. In matters wholly scholastic, reproof and encouragement must be administered together.

Jacques Barzun

William James believed he had found what philosophers most wanted: it was praise. And young men, who are not philosophers, want the same thing or the opportunity to earn it. Setting them tasks they can do, or a little beyond what they can do, is not enough. They must be persuaded that they can learn the sense, and to persuade without coddling; all that is usually necessary is to have the creature recognize that it has lots to jump with. Namely, the means already acquired to be used for the new effort.

Jacques Barzun

"Mans mind, stretched to a new idea, never goes back to its original dimension."

Oliver Wendell Holmes.

It no longer matters as much what I accomplish as that I am in tune with my own sense of belonging to the human race. Self labels are no longer necessary.

Dr. Wayne W. Dyer

I see the facilitation of learning as the aid of education, the way in which we might develop the learning man, the way in which we can learn to live as individuals in process. I see the facilitation of learning as the function, which may hold constructive, tentative, changing, process answers to some of the deepest perplexities, which beset man today.

Carl R. Rogers

The only man who is educated is the man who has learned how to learn; the man who has learned how to adapt and change; the man who has realized that no knowledge is secure, that only the process of seeking knowledge gives a basis for security. Changingness, a reliance on process rather than upon static knowledge, is the only thing that makes any sense as a goal for education in the modern world.

Carl R. Rogers

A long, long time ago George Herbert said: "By all means use sometime to be alone. Salute thyself; see what thy should doth wear." That is good self-renewal doctrine...The individual who has become a stranger to himself has lost the capacity for genuine self-renewal. Niebuhr has written: "the conquest of self is in a sense the inevitable consequence of true self-knowledge." If the self-centered self is shattered by a genuine awareness of it's situation, there is the power of a new life in the experience.

John W. Gardner

After the pupil has been told what serves to make him wiser and better, he must be taught the purpose of logic, physics, geometry, and rhetoric: his judgment once formed he will very soon master which ever branch he may choose.

Schopenhauer

The mind is a strange machine, which can combine the materials offered to it in the most astonishing ways, but without materials from the external world it is powerless.
Bertrand Russell

Happiness lies in the joy of achievement and the thrill of creative effort.
Franklin Roosevelt

Luck is what happens when preparation meets opportunity.
Limer Letterman

Our chief want in life is somebody who will make us do what we can.
Ralph Waldo Emerson

The gods help them that help themselves.
Aesop

Who has self-confidence will lead the rest.
Horace

I am the master of my fate I am the captain of my soul.
W.E. Henley

Knowledge is power.
Francis Bacon.

The life of every teacher is partly dedicated to discovering and encouraging those few powerful minds who will influence our future, and the secret of education is never to forget the possibility, of greatness.
Gilbert Highet

They can do all because they think they can.
Virgil

Time spent on reading and writing, in any subject, is never a waste, and the reward almost always comes, often astonishingly great. The excitement aroused by the discovery that words live is like finding that you can balance on skates. A new world of motion and of feeling is opened out to the student, a source of some anguish balanced by lifelong delight.

Jacques Barzun

When writing a child should select a topic that truly engages his interest.

Jacques Barzun

To know oneself, one should assert oneself.
Albert Camus

The average American would rather be driving a car along a crowded highway than reading a book and thinking. Why this should be so, I cannot tell. It must be something wrong with education. Probably it is the cult of the average: the idea that schools exist in order to make everyone pretty much the same. And that happiness consists in sharing a group life, sweet, humming, undifferentiated, and crowded like bees in a hive.

Gilbert Highet

The first objective of early education should not be training in the reality of the screen by changing channels. Students believes they can as easily alter the world itself, a point made brilliantly by Peter Sellers in the film "Be There."

John R. Silber Pres Boston U.
Speech may 17, 1981
Vital Speeches of the Day

Chance favors the prepared mind.
Louis Pasteur

My hope here is simply to make education appear worthwhile, attractive and attainable to the humblest man.

Albert E. Wiggan

When a subject becomes totally obsolete we make it a required course.

Peter Drucker

The schoolmaster since time immemorial has believed that the ass is an organ of learning. The longer you sit, the more you learn.

Peter Drucker

Now they are converting "progressive" schools into what they call fundamental schools, which are just old-fashioned schools with great emphasis on discipline and the three R's. And much to the consternation of the liberal establishment the kids do better, partly because the parents insist they do better.

Peter Drucker

The purpose of education is to develop self-respect, integrity, confidence, and peace with yourself.

R. V.E.

Tis education forms the common mind, just as the twig is bent, the trees inclined.

Alexander Pope

Education has for it's object the formation of character.

Herbert Spencer

Education is what survives when what has been learnt has been forgotten.

B.F. Skinner

Training is everything. The peach was once a bitter almond; cauliflower is nothing but cabbage with a college education.
Mark Twain

One must learn by doing the thing; though you think you know it, you have not certainly until you try.
Sophocles

In school you are measured against an arbitrary standard and judged by how far you fell short of the standard. If you came up only 3 percent short, you got a 97 and a C. The feedback system-which told you how well you performed was based on negatives. The system encouraged you to avoid the penalties of failure, rather than seek the rewards of excellence.
Dr. James E. Loehr and
Peter J. McLaughlin

Men can starve from a lack of self-realization as much as they can from a lack of bread.
Richard Wright
Native Son

Crafty men have contempt for studies; simple men admire them; and wise men use them: for they teach not their own use; but that is a wisdom without them and about them, won by observation.
Francis Bacon

Never depend on anyone except yourself.
La. Fontaine

A little learning is a dangerous thing.
Alexander Pope.

It is only when knowledge is found for her own sake that she gives rich and unexpected gifts in any abundance to her servants.
Roger Bacon

Four chief sources of ignorance he denounced: respect for authority, custom, the sense of the ignorant crowd, and the vain proud unteachableness of our dispositions.
Roger Bacon

I have sworn upon the altar of God, "eternal hostility against every form of tyranny over the mind of man."
Thomas Jefferson

It's what you learn after you know it all the counts.
John Wooden

I know now that my circumstances do not make me what I am, but that they reveal who I have chosen to be.
Dr. Wayne W Dyer

I call a complete and generous education that which fits a man to perform, justly, skillfully, and magnanimously, at the offices both private and public of peace and war.
Milton

The direction in which education starts a man will determine his future life.
Plato

"What the eye never sees the heart never longs for," is an Irish proverb with immense truth in this whole region of education. It enforces the importance of environment, the value of a rich and varied treatment of a child's dawning faculties, opening up possibilities in different lines till one day the soul may wake and grow.
Hugh Black

Who supplies another with a constructive thought has enriched him forever.
AlfredA. Montapert

Jefferson said, "Power must always go back to the people." In education power must always go back to the student. Adults should make a serious effort to make it easy for students to learn at their own speed. That means, rather than stifle their efforts, they need all the freedom we have the courage to give them.
R. V. E.

Education becomes the release of human possibilities.
John W.Gardner

Fit examples can be chosen for all the most profitable teachings of philosophy to which human action ought to be referred, as to a standard. Our pupils should be told: What is right to desire, what hard-earned money is useful for, how much should be bestowed on country and dear kindred, what sort of man, God intended you to be, and for what place in the commonwealth he maked you out... what we are and what life we are born to lead. What it is to know and not to know, what the aim of his study should be; what courage, temperance, and justice are; what the difference is between ambition and greed, servitude and submission, license and liberty; by what signs one may recognize genuine and solid contentment, to what extent we should fear death, suffering, and shame, and how to avoid or endure each kind of hardship. What springs we move; and the reason for all the different impulses within us.

For it seems to me that the first ideas which his mind should be made to absorb must be those that relate his behavior and morals, that teach him to know himself, and to know how to die well and live well
Schopenhauer

To travel hopefully is a better thing than to arrive.
Stevenson

Learning once made popular is no longer learning; it has the appearance of something, which we have bestowed upon ourselves, as the dew appears to rise from the field which it refreshes.
Johnson

Education is seen to be more than a mere brain development; it is the total forming of a human being, physical, intellectual, moral, and spiritual.
Hugh Black

If the relation of education to the mind is like that of food to the body, we do not often take anything like the same care to give the mind its right food as we do to nourish the body.
Hugh Black

I find that one of the best, but most difficult, ways for me to learn is to drop my own defensiveness, at least temporarily, and to try to understand the way in which his experience seems and feels to the other person.
Carl Rogers

A boy may be brilliant mathematician... at the age of thirteen. But, I never know a child of the age who had much that was useful to say about the ends of human life.
Robert M. Hutchins

The moment the little boy is concerned with which is a jay and which is a sparrow, he can no longer see the birds or hear them sing.
Eric Berne

One should be able to sense the beauty of the rhythm of life to appreciate, as we do in grand symphonies, its main theme, its strains of conflict and the final resolution. The movements of these cycles are very much the same in a normal life, but the music must be provided by the individual himself. In some souls, the discordant note becomes harsher and harsher and finally overwhelms or submerges the main melody. Sometimes the discordant note gains so much power that the music can no longer go on, and the individual shoots himself with a pistol or jumps into river. But that is because his original leit-motif has been hopelessly over-shadowed through the lack of a good self-education. Otherwise the normal human life runs to its normal end in a kind of dignified movement and procession.

Lin Yutang

The Importance of living

It is important that adults create an atmosphere in which the children can grow in freedom without fear.

J. Krishnamurti

We pay a heavy price for our fear of failure. It is a powerful obstacle to growth. It assumes the progressive rearranging of the personality and prevents exploration and experimentation. There is no learning, without some difficulties and fumbling. If you want to keep on learning, you must keep on risking failure-all of your life. It's as simple as that. When Max Planck was awarded the Nobel Prize he said: "Looking back... over the long and labyrinthine path which finally led to the discovery (of the quantum theory). I am, vividly reminded of Goethes' saying that men will always be making mistakes as long as they are striving for something.

John W. Gardner

Children are not born human; they are made so.

Jacques Barzun

To know by heart is not to know; it is to retain what we have given our memory to keep. What we know rightly we dispose of, without looking at the model, without turning our eye towards our books. Sad competence, a purely bookish competence! I intend it to serve as decoration, not as foundation, according to the opinion of Plato, who says that steadfastness, faith, and sincerity are the real philosophy.
Moniaigne

For doubting pleases me no less than knowing.
Dante

Education should be as gradual as the moonrise, perceptible not in progress but in result.
George John Melville

Perhaps the most valuable result of all education is the ability to make yourself do the thing you have to do, when it ought to be done, whether you like it or not; it is the first lesson that ought to be learned; and however early a man's training begins, it is probably the last lesson that he learns thoroughly.
Thomas H. Huxley

Jefferson said, "Power must always go back to the people." In education I say-power must always go back to the student. I think adults should make a serious effort to make it easy for students to learn at their own speed. That means, rather than stifle their efforts, they need all the freedom we have the courage to give them.
R. V.E.

We shall solve very few of our problems if we turn our backs on the rational methods that education provides.
Charles Frankel

If you have education-chance and accident have less influence on your life. You can guide your own destiny.

Charles Frankel

One of the most difficult problems we face is to make it possible for young people to participate in the great tasks of their time.

John W. Gardner

The man who has ceased to learn ought not to be allowed to wander around loose in these dangerous days.

M.M.Coady.

Surely the worst of the evils are the evils of the learned, and surely the best of good is the good of the learned.

Arabian Proverb.

He who learns but does not think is lost; he who thinks but does not learn is in danger.

Confucius.

Whoso neglects learning in his youth loses the past and is dead for the future.

Euripides.

One pound of learning requires ten pounds of commonsense to apply it.

Perssian Proverb.

CHAPTER 9

QUOTATIONS

EXCELLENCE

One's destiny is determined, not by what he possesses, but by what possesses him.
Ancient proverb

Few things are impossible to diligence and skill.
Samuel Johnson

All the world loves a winner, and has no time for a loser.
Knute Rockne

Each honest calling, each walk of life, has its own elite, its own aristocracy based on excellence of performance.
James Bryant Conant

How much better it is to be envied than pitied.
Herodotus

Nothing in human life is more to be lamented, than that a wise man should have so little influence.
Herodotus

Day by day fix your eyes upon the greatness of Athens, until you become filled with the love of her; and when you are impressed by the spectacle of her glory, reflect that this empire has been acquired by men who knew their duty and had the courage to do it.
Thucydides

We come from a world where we have known incredible standards of excellence, and we dimly remember beauties which we have not seized again.
Thornton N. Wilder

There is nothing so fatal to character as half-finished tasks.
David Lloyd George

Get action. Do things; be sane, don't fritter away your time; create, act, take a place wherever you are and be somebody; get action.
Theodore Roosevelt

When you are aspiring to the highest place, it is honorable to reach the second or even the third rank.
Cicero

It is not because things are difficult that we do not dare to attempt them, but they are difficult because we do not dare to do so.
Seneca

Act so as to elicit the best in others and thereby in thyself.
Felix Adler

The hero is no braver than an ordinary man, but he is brave five minutes longer.
Ralph Waldo Emerson

He who trusts all things to chance, makes a lottery of his life.
Ancient proverb

Circumstances! I make circumstances!
Napoleon Bonaparte

By mutual confidence and mutual aid, great deeds are done, and great discoveries made.
Homer

What we have to do is to be forever curiously testing new opinions and courting new impressions.
Waiter Pater

There are three marks of a superior man: being virtuous, he is free from anxiety; being wise, he is free from perplexity; being brave, he is free from fear.
Confucius.

It is a wretched taste to be gratified with mediocrity when the excellent lies before us.
Isaac D'Israeli.

There can be no excess to love, to knowledge, to beauty, when these attributes are considered in the purest sense.
Ralph Waldo Emerson.

How glorious it is--and also how painful--to be an exception.
Louis Charles

Those who attain to any excellence commonly spend life in some one single pursuit, for excellence is not often gained upon easier terms.
Samuel Johnson.

The pursuit of excellence is less profitable than the pursuit of bigness, but it can be more satisfying.
David Mackenzie Ogilvy.

All things excellent are as difficult as they are rare.
Baruch Spinoza.

He who stops being better, stops being good.
Oliver Cromwell.

One that desires to excel should endeavor it in those things that are in themselves most excellent.
Epictetus.

There is no excellency without difficulty.
Ovid.

I tell you that as long as I can conceive something better than myself I cannot be easy unless I am striving to bring it into existence or clearing the way for it.
George Bernard Shaw.

Each excellent thing, once learned, serves for a measure of all other knowledge.
Sir Philip Sidney.

Everyone expects to go further than his father went; everyone expects to be better than he was born and every generation has one big impulse in its heart-to exceed all the other generations of the past in all the things that make life worth living.
William Allen White.

FEELINGS

Our feelings are similar to the radar used by a ship that is crossing the ocean. They give us constant feedback, which tells us if there are obstacles, and they help guide the direction we are going. Of course, we can't be foolish, we can't live entirely by our feelings. It's important that we keep our conscience clear, that we have good manners so we fit comfortably in society. We must take care of our responsibilities; and we must maintain a disciplined focus on ourselves so we don't fall off the path that leads us to the main goals of our life.

When our feelings, are written down, they help us keep score. They tell us where we are today and help us decide where we want to go tomorrow. They help us set new goals for a new day. We should expect confidence, competence, and success.

Our feelings will help us grab a hold of every opportunity to wrestle with problems that are directly in front of us. It takes courage to act on intuitive feelings.   I like the feeling that I am moving ahead every day, eventually to that thing called wisdom, whatever it may be. Montaigne said, his whole purpose in life was to use all of the God given talent and ability he has.

Socrates said, "Know-thyself."   Use of our talent, our ability, our knowledge of our self, all come from sensitive listening, to the feelings we have. The more sophisticated and educated we are, the less likely we are to express strong feelings openly. We have too high a stake in remaining rational at all times, even under stress. Although it makes no sense many people try to pay as little attention to their feelings as they can, hoping that somehow this might lessen their effect. We still tend to hide even from...(ourselves) the fact that many of life's most important choices and decisions are made on the basis of feeling, not rationally."

The entire educational process is geared toward thinking, even if it fails to produce many truly thoughtful individuals. Having such a heavy investment in rationality we obviously want to assure its safety. We do so in strange and ineffective ways.

Reuven Bar-Levav. M.D.
Thinking in the Shadow of Feelings. p. 119

It is the state of feeling great that produces great performance.
Dr. James E. Loehr.
Peter J. McLaughlin.

If you think feeling good is a result of doing well, you've got it backward. Thanks to the configuration of the human nervous system, the emotions have to be in place first.
Dr. James E. Loehr.
Peter J. McLaughlin.
Mentally Tough   p.16

The common division of the mental powers is into feeling, knowing, willing; but while the distinction is a real one and can be truly and usefully made, it is only a distinction in function. The three states are never completely separated, but intermingle with each other.
Hugh Black

The first and most important step toward success is the feeling that we can succeed.
Nelson Boswell

To love what you do and feel that it matters-how could anything be more fun.
Katharine Graham

Poetry is the language of feeling.
W. Winter

You have a remarkable ability, which you never acknowledged before. It is to look at a situation and know whether you can do it. And I mean really know the answer.

Carl Frederick

Whatever I do without feeling has no value.

Anais Nin

What we feel is as true a fact as what we think.

Hugh Black

The life of the heart is what makes up the individuality of each of us more than even our distinctive intellectual powers.

Hugh Black

Through this journal process of expression and reflection they discover new solutions to problems, enter into and appreciate the process of their lives, and exercise their creative capacities. They experience first hand how the qualities they most enjoy in their writing-spontaneity, honesty, depth, clarity, ambiguity, humor, and feelings-agree also with the qualities of a mature, self-aware person. They develop their creativity simply by developing themselves.

Tristine Rainer

Do you reveal your feelings fully or hide them even from yourself!

Tristine Rainer
The New Diary. p. 272

While rereading for feelings you need to distinguish between affected or overly dramatized writing and vulnerable, honest writing. If you sound like the reporter of your emotional experience rather than its source, it may indicate distance or a fear of our feelings. If your writing seems to you weak in genuine feelings you might ask yourself when you write, "what did I feel?

What do I feel now? How do I really feel about the person, place or thing? You might try to allow yourself to feel vulnerable as you write, permit cathartic writing, and work with your dreams in the diary.

Tristine Rainer
The New Diary. p 281

Human Beings are complex, not simple. For example, they think but they also feel. The relationship of thinking and feeling is interactional and cyclical. The way I structure my world makes me feel about it in certain ways.

The way I feel affects what I pay attention to and how I make sense of it.

Alien F.Harrison
Robert M. Bramson, Ph. D
Styles of Thinking

Honesty is letting other people know how you feel about them.

Habits of the Heart. P. 101

Whitman believed that a life of strong feelings was a successful life. The expressive and deep feeling's was a successful life. The expressive and deeply feeling self becomes the source of life.

Habits of the Heart. p. 34

Mark Twain said, "Something moral is something you feel good about.

Freud surrendered himself not only to impulse but also to the demands of the material he worked on "Freud as a Writer."

Patrick J. Mahony

I guess, if there is anyone who needs to owe anybody anything, it is honesty in letting each other know how they feel about each other, and that if feelings change, to be open and receptive, to accept those changes, knowing that people in a relationship are not cement."

Habits of the Heart p. 101

Ted Oster feels that communication and the sharing of feelings are at the heart of a good marriage. And relationships require work. "You can't have something as good as a love relationship without putting a lot of effort into it. It's a wonderful thing, but it's not going to keep going by itself just because it's wonderful.

Habits of the Heart. p. 104

It is a well known fact that emotion or feeling rules the majority of people.

Napoleon Hill

I will listen to anyone's convictions, but pray keep your doubts to yourself.

Goethe

We know the truth, not only by reason, but also by the heart.
Blaise Pascal

Every human feeling is greater and larger than its exciting cause-a proof, I think, that man is designed for a higher state of existence.

Samuel Taylor Coleridge.

Emotions become more violent when expression is stifled.
Philo.

Feeling does not become stronger in the religious life by waiting, but by using it.

Henry Ward Beecher.

Richard V. Eastman

Our feelings were given us to excite to action, and when they end in themselves, they are cherished to no good purpose.
Daniel Keyte Sandford.

By starving emotions we become humorless, rigid and stereotyped; by repressing them we become literal, reformatory and holier-than-thou; encouraged, they perfume life; discouraged, they poison it.
Joseph Collins.

Emotion is not something shameful, subordinate, second-rate; it is a supremely valid phase of humanity at its noblest and most mature.
Joshua Loth Liebman.

All loving emotions, like plants, shoot up most rapidly in the tempestuous atmosphere of life.
Jean Paul Richter.

A loving heart is the truest wisdom.
Charles John Huffman Dickens.

Only feeling understands feeling.
Heinrich Heine.

FREEDOM

Teenagers need freedom to explore their world. Responsibility is a safe way for them to stretch their wings, make mistakes and discover how too fall without doing too much harm to them selves. A useful lesson in the question of Freedom is: "Why do immigrants come to America?"   Freedom. Management has to eliminate barriers to people experiencing joy in their work and has to encourage each to develop himself.
W. Edwards Deming.
Dr. Deming by Rafael Aguayo

A good organization is hardly felt and hardly seen. If it is seen and felt, it is most likely the source of problems and therefore the source of loss for both employees and clients.

W. Edwards Deming.

Dr. Deming by Rafael Aguayo

To start out with the question "What should I contribute?" gives freedom. It gives freedom because it gives responsibility to all who have the courage to ask the question..

W. Edwards Deming.

Dr. Deming by Rafael Aguayo.

On-the-job-improvement can take place when fear is eliminated......when the "us-against-you" attitude is eliminated...... when freedom-too-speak-up gets involved employees involved in the search for quality.

Dr. W. Edwards Deming.

GOALS

I go and look at a stonecutter hammering away at his rock perhaps a hundred times without as much as a crack, showing in it. Yet at the hundred and first blow it will split in two, and I know it was not that blow that did it-but all that had gone before.

Jacob Riis

There's no thrill in easy sailing when the skies are clear and blue, there's no joy in merely doing things which any one can do. But there is some satisfaction that is mighty sweet to take, when you reach a destination that you thought you'd never make.

Spirelly

A great pleasure in life is doing what people say you cannot do.

Waiter Gagehot

Things may come to those who wait, but only things left by those who hustle.
Abraham Lincoln

Obstacles are those frightful things you see when you take your eyes off your goals.

Don't wait for your ship to come in, swim out to it.

You will become as small as your controlling desire' as great as your dominant aspiration.
James Allen

Far away there in the sunshine are my highest aspirations. I may not reach them, but I can look up and see their beauty, believe in them and try to follow where they lead.
Louisa May Alcott

Chance favors the prepared mind.
Louis Pasteur

The future belongs to those who believe in the beauty of their dreams.
Eleanor Roosevelt

If you have built castles in the air, your work need not be lost; that is where they should be. Now put the foundations under them.
Thoreau

It takes courage to push yourself to places that you have never been before, to test your limits, to break through barriers. People seldom improve when they have no other model but themselves to copy after.
Goldsmith

Real leaders are ordinary people with extraordinary determination.

The only time you can't afford to fail is the last time you try.
Charles Kettering

Paralyze resistance with persistence.
Woody Hayes

If you've made up your mind you can do something, you've absolutely right. Do not let what you cannot do interfere with what you can do.
John Wooden

Most people give up just when they're about to achieve success. They quit on the one-yard-line. They give up at the last minute of the game one-foot from a winning touchdown.
H. Ross Perot

So much does the soul require an object at which to aim, that when it does not have one, it will turn to violence upon itself, and create false and fantastic problems, in something to work upon.
Montaigne

People with goals succeed because they know where they're going.
Earl Nightingale

I reach my goals by, "following my bliss."
Deanis Francis Mills

It sometimes seems that intense desire creates not only its own opportunities, but its own talents.
Eric Hoffer

A strong passion for any subject will ensure success, for the desire of the end will point out the means.
William Hazlitt

> They have no magic to stir man's
> blood and probably themselves will not
> be realized.
> Make big plans; aim high
> in hope and work,
> Remembering that a noble
> logical diagram.
> Once recorded will not die.
> Daniel H. Burnham

Perpetual devotion to what a man calls his business is only to be sustained by perpetual neglect of many other things.
Stevenson

It is better to be a fool than to be dead.
Stevenson

Most sales people aim to sell but never pull the trigger.
Paul Siegler

Make a habit of visualizing your dream as already accomplished. Be specific see your work completed. Then write down your goals. Answer these questions: Where do I want to be a year from now? Five years from now? Ten years from now? There is something almost magical about making the commitment on paper.
Deanie F. Mills

You've got to think about the "big thing," while you're doing small things., so that all the small things go in the right direction.
Alvin Toffler

"There is one lone reason," he said in a speech, "why I am here today. I dreamed. I dreamed that someday I would be here, telling you how I, Victor Frankl, had survived the Nazi concentration camps. I've never been here before, I've never seen any of you before, I've never given this speech before. But in my dreams, in my dreams, I have stood before you and said these words a thousand times." Dream on...
Harvey Mackay

If you don't have a destination, you'll never get there.
Harvey Mackay

"Most of us are seat of the pants, one day at a time operators. Our goals are fuzzy and our plans for achieving them non-existent.
Harvey Mackay

IBM's basic plan for achieving the company's goals consists of three simple parts: respect for the individual, whether it's a customer, employee, or supplier; pursuit of excellence; and outstanding customer service.
Harvey Mackay

"A goal is a dream with a deadline." Write yours down because that's the only way you'll give them the substance they need to force you to carry them out.
Harvey Mackay.

Human survival itself very often depends on a kind of future vision, seeing ones self in specific situations as a healthy thriving, creative person.

Harvey Mackay

The starting point of all achievement is desire. Keep this constantly in mind. Weak desire brings weak results, just as a small amount of fire makes a small amount of heat.

Napoleon Hill

For the resolute and determined there is time and opportunity.

Ralph Waldo Emerson

High aims form high character, and great objects bring out great minds.

Tryon Edwards.

Aim at the sun, and you may not reach it; but your arrow will fly far higher than if aimed at an object on a level with yourself.

Joel Hawes.

Not failure, but low aim, is crime.
James Russell Lowell.

In great attempts it is glorious even to fail.
Longinus.

Have a purpose in life, and having it, throw into your work such strength of mind and muscle as God has given you.

Thomas Carlyle.

Many good purposes and intentions lie in the graveyard.
Philip Henry

GROWTH

The only limit to our realization of tomorrow will be our doubts of today.
Franklin D. Roosevelt

Most men are old fogies at twenty-five because they have ceased to grow.
William James

The highest reward for a person's toil is not what they get for it, but what they become by it.
John Ruskin

I find the great thing in this world is not so much where we stand as in what direction we are moving.
Oliver Wendell Holmes

When you cease to dream you cease to live.
Malcolm S. Forbes

William James said, "Genius means little more than the faculty of perceiving in an inhabitable way." By the time we reach adulthood, we are driven as much by habit as by anything else, and there is infinity of habits in us. From the woman who twirls a strand of hair when she's nervous or bored to the man who expresses his insecurity by never saying "thank you," We are all victims of habits. They do not merely rule us, they inhibit us and make fools of us.

To free ourselves from habit, to resolve the paradoxes, to transcend conflicts, to become the master rather than the slaves of our own lives, we must first see and remember, and then forget. That is why true learning begins with unlearning and why unlearning is one of the recurring themes of our story.

Every great inventor or scientist has had to unlearn conventional wisdom in order to proceed with his work. For example, conventional wisdom said, "If God had meant man to fly, he would have given him wings." But the Wright brothers disagreed and built an airplane.

No one, not your parents nor your teachers nor your peers-can teach you how to be yourself.
Warren Bennis
On Becoming a Leader p. 69

When one has the opportunity to fight for his beliefs, it is a true joy. As we grow and begin to understand ourselves we find that we are more able to heir, and nourish others.
The first thing a good pitcher needs is a thirst for knowledge. Any pitcher afraid to try something new for fear of failing will fail for lack of enough pitches to keep him in the big leagues. Every day a pro pitcher at some level is warned that if he does not come up with another wrinkle to expand his repertoire, he'll soon be shipped out.
Orel Hershiser

Complacency is death. Start thinking you've got it licked, and you're finished.
Orel Hershiser

You train yourself to do more than just cope; coping is for beginners. Mental toughness is for winners.
Dr. James E. Loehr and Peter J. McLaughlin
Menially Tough p. 10

Growth is not focusing on what was, but on what might be.
Tom Peters
Thriving on Chaos   p. 54

We all change and grow very slowly. It's like a trip across the ocean with a shoreline that never seems to move. You can't see improvement in yourself if all you see is the reflection of yourself in the water.
Schopenhauer
Essays and Aphorisms p. 69

You will grow, you can't help it. You will be a better person ten years from now. But it doesn't just happen; you have to make it happen. Habit is the essential mechanism of living. To habit all recurrent activities are committed, so that intelligence may be freed for new and important tasks. Habit does not exist to control intelligence, not to supplant intelligence. It exists to do the mechanical work so that the intelligence may be free.
Joseph K Hart.
The Discovery of Intelligence

The human mind must be used as it is meant to be; for the cause of human growth and integrity.
Norman Cousins
Human Options. p 122

Consistency, mediocrity, requires you to be as ignorant today as you were a year ago.
Bernard Berenson

Socrates said, "The unexamined life is not worth living." I'd do a step further: The unexamined life is impossible to live successfully. Like oarsmen, we generally move forward while looking backward, but not until we truly see the past, truly under stand it, can we truly move forward, and upward. Until you make your life your own, you're walking around in borrowed clothes.
Warren Bennis

All genuine progress results from finding new facts.
Wheeler Mcmillen

Personal growth, in my opinion, requires that you feel better about yourself today than you did yesterday. You must have respect for yourself. You cannot carry the weight of yesterday's problems around on your shoulders. Be kind to yourself by forgiving yourself for the mistakes you have made. But, don't be weak, be disciplined, tough, and aggressive. Work on a goal that "sounds to you" like personal growth. You can do anything that comes to your mind, but only if you slowly grow, "into it."
R.V.E

The lack of intimacy with one's self and consequently with others is what created the loneliest and most alienated people in the world. Progress ultimately proves that "the process of growth in a human being, the process out of which a person emerges, is essentially an inward process."
Anais Nin
In Favor of the Sensitive Man.

What is personal growth? Where did that term come from? At my age personal growth is what I did not have when I was very young; in my twenties and thirties. I'm beginning to feel very capable, secure, able, to handle any kind of problem. I'm excited about change. I enjoy learning. I have more interests now than I had when young.

I'm beginning to feel like, maybe; someday I will get my act together. I'm not there yet, but I'm feeling the outer edges of wisdom. I'm hoping, striving for more. It's like being in a whirlpool of water; I can see the hole in the middle. The feeling of picking up speed as I get closer and closer to the middle, moving in on the goal with increasing excitement. I'm often naive, even vulnerable. I'm not worried about mistakes, only about not doing all that can be done.
R. V.E.

"Finding oneself" is not something one does alone. The quest for personal growth and self-fulfillment is supposed to lead one into relationships with others and most important among them are love and marriage.

Habits of the Heart p. 85.

Right ethics are central and go from the soul outward. Gift is contrary to the law of the universe. Serving others is serving us.

Emerson

An ethical teacher who gives freely always learns more than the students.

A man should never be ashamed to own he has been in the wrong, which is but saying, in other words, that he is wiser today than he was yesterday.

Alexander Pope

Trees and fields tell me nothing: men are my teachers.

Plato

Who are your friends? Do they believe in you? Or do they stunt your growth with ridicule and disbelief? If the latter, you haven't friends. Go find some.

Ray Bradbury.

I have not so much thought my way through life as done things and found what it was and who I was after the doing. Each tale I wrote was a way of finding selves. Each self found each day slightly different from the one found twenty-four hours earlier.

Ray Bradbury.

Everybody wants to be somebody, but nobody wants to grow.

Johann Wolfgang von Goethe.

A man's growth is seen in the successive choirs of his friends.
Ralph Waldo Emerson.

Undertake something that is difficult; it will do you good. Unless you try to do something beyond what you have already mastered, you will never grow.
Ronald E. Osborn.

We want our children to grow up to be such persons that ill-fortune, if they meet with it, will bring out strength in them, and that good fortune will not trip them up, but make them winners.
Edward Sandford Martin.

Great occasions do not make heroes or cowards; they simply unveil them to the eyes of men. Silently and imperceptibly, as we wake or sleep, we grow strong or we grow weak, and at last some crisis shows us what we have become.
Bishop Westcott.

HEALTH

To say that health is a condition of a man's efficiency is more than to say that it will probably lead to success in his business. It should help to make him a man of a more all-round character, since character is formed, as Goethe said, in the stream of the world.
Hugh Black

A man who is physically fit is surely all the better citizen.
Hugh Black.

Aerobic exercise performed regularly is natures best physiological tranquilizer." Amen!
Dr. Kenneth Cooper M.D

Running is for me a reaffirmation . I am here. I run because I am me.

Joseph Goodman
A 78 year old runner
Fifty-plus Runners Assoc.

There is a great deal of scientific evidence which virtually guarantees that we will feel better if we exercise daily.

Keith Johnsgard, Ph. D
Fifty-Plus Runners Assoc.

The highest function of life can only be adequately performed in health.

Hugh Black

What we need is the right view of the whole subject, which will make us treat the body sanely and reverently as an integral part of life.

Hugh Black

The greatest writers impress us with a sense of the healthy vigour and sanity of their mind. With them we are in a large world, under wide skies, and amid wholesome life. There is no feeling of depressed vitality about them or their work. The morbid and diseased and the tragic side of the world have their place in their interpretation of human life, but always in the natural proportion and from the point of view that health is the normal. Clear vision, and keen insight, and true feeling, and productive energy in all forms of art depend on conditions of health of body and mind and soul.

Hugh Black

The duty of a wise care for health is bigger than merely adding an important asset for personal happiness. To a large extent it determines the efficiency of our lives. Its results are seen all along the line, giving a bias to our views and affecting our capacity to work and the quality of our work. Students especially sometimes forget that the brain can be overtaxed, and like an over-bent bow may never quite recover from the strain. It often demands from the student great control, and what looks like sacrifice, for him to rigorously follow the rules of health, such as attention to diet and sleep and exercise.

Hugh Black

"Courage and hope and trust have a conquering efficacy over some bodily ailments and over some nervous states of mind, while doubt and fear reduce vitality, we know even more certainly the converse side that states of body, influence the higher life in all its activities. The common man's philosophy is usually the fruit of his physical temperament. Most optimism's can be traced to a good digestion, and most pessimisms to dyspepsia."

Hugh Black

The Greek passion for gymnastic, or what we would call athletics, finds some justification from the facts of life. What the precise connection is between the body and the higher life we need not try to discover, whether in the ultimate issues character depends on the physical nature, or whether the body is the expression of the soul.

Hugh Black.

A merry heart make a cheerful countenance. Peace of mind a good conscience, a gentle, generous, unselfish heart are all great elements of health, just as anger and excessive grief and hatred tend to destroy vitality.

Hugh Black

A happy mood of mind, a sweet and simple piety, a generous desire to help and serve others will encourage and strengthen health in ourselves.

Hugh Black

182

We may sometimes think that the cult of athletics is in danger of being carried too far among us, but it is nothing compared to the practice of the Greeks. To them it was almost a half of human education. Every town had its gymnasium, its baths, its racing-track, on a scale hardly conceivable by us. Training of the body was so fit and about scientific principles, not haphazardly as sports for the pastime of children or as exhibitions for the amusement of spectators. Philosophers gravely reasoned out the due proportion. Which athletic development should have in the ideal education? Even Plato in his scheme of education sets apart exclusively for "gymnastic" the years of a young man's life which seem to us the most essential of establishing moral character and intellectual pursuits-those between seventeen and twenty. It was because he took long views of life that he was willing to make this sacrifice of those most precious years. He believed that it would pay afterwards both morally and intellectually.

The many references, casual though they are, scattered through the New Testament itself give us some indication of the place the gymnastic art held in Greek life. The New Testament never throws contempt on the body, but recommends a wise and sane treatment of it, and even when advocating a higher kind of discipline does not denounce bodily training. It has its uses, it asserts, though these can only be partial, having reference only to one department of a mans nature.

All who saw the results could not but admire the perfection of strength and beauty and health which was the result of the classic training. Every competitor at these great contests, every one who entered for a race or for a boxing match, did so after the most careful training and the most stringent discipline. "Even, man that striveth for the mastery is temperate in all things. " says the Apostle, asking from his readers for something of the same eager interest and willing sacrifice in the higher race and the nobler fight of life.   .

Hugh Black

We need true proportional development, concurrent growth in the different directions open to us, physical, mental, moral, spiritual.

Hugh Black

He who has health has hope, and he who has hope has everything.

Arbabian Proverb.

True enjoyment comes from activity of the mind and exercise of the body; the two are united.

Alexander von Humboldt.

CHAPTER 10

QUOTATIONS

HUMOR

Humor starts very early and is a remarkable asset indeed, especially if given free reign and supported to full development. I have seen remarkable evidence of this asset in children only two years of age. Their perception, their sensitivity to incongruities and ironies, and their capacity for responsive fun and humorous invention, too, was already in much evidence. A sense of humor as with other assets requires development. These beginnings in childhood grow to fuller and deeper fruition as life experiences increase. A sense of humor requires high development and use of intellect, emotion, and creativity in order to grow and to be sustained. But I speak here of the real adult thing in which humor is much more than mechanically repeated lines but is rather the product of spontaneous invention.

A highly developed sense of humor does not disappear even in severe depression. I have seen evidence of it in many people who were for the moment very sick. As a clinician I view this asset as one of the most hopeful prognostic signs. It always indicates a quick and inventive mind of a high ability to make abstractions. It is nearly always evidence of at least some insight about people and an indication of at least some experience of real relating with people. It is often the first aspect of the patient I can use in reaching him or her quickly so as to neutralize a crisis situation; properly used by therapist and patient, this asset can be lifesaving. A sense of humor is invariably enormously useful in relating to others, the world, and ourselves generally. It serves as an important form of communication. It makes the most difficult experiences bearable. It increases humility, helping us to take ourselves seriously without pretentious solemnity.

Children in whom this valuable asset was not snuffed out are fortunate indeed. Those in whom it has been fostered and for whom it has flourished are blessed with an extremely vital human inner resource that will serve them well all of their lives. Even as we take ourselves and the world seriously, humor helps to reduce solemnity, pretense, affectation, and the pain of realistic difficulties.

Theordore Isaac Rubin, M.D.
Child Potential p. 51

Paradise for a happy man lies in his own good nature.
EdwardAbbey

If I had no sense of humor, I would long ago have committed suicide.
Gandhi

There is certainly no defense against adverse fortune which is, on the whole, so effectual as a habitual sense of humor.
Thomas Higginson.

A man isn't poor if he can still laugh.
Raymond Hitchcock.

Good humor is goodness and wisdom combined.
Owen Meredith.

Good humor isn't a trait of character, it is an art which requires practice.
David Seabury.

Good humor is one of the best articles of dress one can wear in society.
William Thackeray.

The best sense of humor belongs to the person who can laugh at himself. Humor is like a needle and thread--deftly used it can patch up just about everything.

INDIVIDUALISM

Genius is the ability to reduce the complicated to the simple.
C. W. Ceran

The mould of a man's fortune is in his own hands.
Francis Bacon

If a man is called to be a street sweeper, he should sweep streets even as Michelangelo painted, or Beethoven composed music, or Shakespeare wrote poetry. He should sweep streets so well that all the hosts of heaven and earth will pause to say, here live a great street sweeper who did his job well.
Martin Luther King. Jr.

One hour of life, crowded to the full with glorious action, and filled with noble risks, is worth whole years of those mean observances of paltry decorum, in which men steal through existence, like sluggish waters through a marsh, without either honour of observation.
Sir Waiter Scott

I do the best I know how, the very best I can; and I mean to keep on doing it to the end. If the end brings me out all right, what is said against me will not amount to anything. If the end brings me out all wrong, ten angels swearing I was right would make no difference.

Abraham Lincoln

Destiny is not a matter of chance, it is a matter of choice.

Great, genuine and extraordinary work can be done only in so far as its author disregards the method, the thoughts, the opinions of his contemporaries, and quietly works on, in spite of their criticism, on his side despising what they praise. No one becomes great without arrogance of this sort. He must listen to himself-be true to himself.

Shopenhauer

Great spirits have always encountered violent opposition from mediocre minds.

Albert Einstein

The Winner-is always part of the answer;
The Loser-is always part of the problem;
The Winner-is always has a program;
The Loser- always has an excuse;
The Winner- says "Let me do it for you;"
The Loser- says "That's not my job."
The Winner-sees an answer for every problem;
The Loser- sees a problem for every answer;
The Winner- sees a green near every green trap;
The Loser- sees two or three sand traps near every green;
The Winner- says, "It may be difficult but it's possible;"
The Loser-says, "It may be possible but it's too difficult."
Be A Winner

The golden opportunity you are seeking is in yourself. It is not in your environment; it is not in luck, or chance, or the help of others it is in yourself alone.
Orison Swet Marden

Hold yourself responsible for a higher standard than any body else expects you. Never excuse yourself.
Henry Ward Beecher

You see things; and you say, "Why?" But I dream things that never were; and I say, "Why not?"
George Bernard Shaw

A great pleasure in life is doing what people say you cannot do.
Waller Gagehot

Nothing is harder in the whole human condition than to achieve a full sense of identity-than to know who you are, where you are going and what you mean to live and die for.
Arthur M. Schlesinger, Jr.

William H. Whyte, Jr., has described the rise of "the organization man" working by day in immense business concerns, sleeping by night in immense suburban developments, deriving his fantasy life from mass-produced entertainments, spending his existence, not as an individual, but as a member of a group and coming in the end to feel guilty and lost when he deviates from his fellows. Adjustment rather than achievement become the social ideal. Men no longer fulfill an inner sense of what they must be; indeed, with the cult of the group, that inner sense itself begins to evaporate. Identity consists, not of self-realization, but of smooth absorption into the group.
Arthur M. Schlesinger, Jr.

Richard V. Eastman

Far better it is to dare mighty things, to win glorious triumphs, even though checkered by failure, than to take rank with those poor spirits who neither enjoy much nor suffer much, because they live in the gray twilight that knows not victory nor defeat.

Theodore Roosevelt

The man who wins may have been counted out several times, but he didn't hear the referee.

H.E. Jansen

One of the pleasantest things in the world is going a journey; but I like to go by myself.

William Hazlit

The soul of a journey is liberty, perfect liberty; to think, feel, do just as one pleases.

William Hazlitt

I do not believe it useful to generalize opinions, to teach admirations. It is for each man to procure himself the emotion he needs, and the morality, which suits him.

Remy De Gourmont

A beautiful woman by the name of Peace Pilgim walked across this country a few years back, spreading her message of peace and love and personal transformation. She described the characteristics of personal transformation in this short list.

Some Signs and Symptoms of Inner Peace

A tendency to think and act spontaneously rather than on fears based on past experiences.

An unmistakable ability to enjoy each moment.

A loss of interest in judging other people

A loss of interest in interpreting the actions of others.

A loss of interest in conflict

A loss of the ability to worry

Frequent, overwhelming episodes of appreciation

Contended feeling of connectedness with others and nature

Frequent attacks of smiling

An increased susceptibility to love extended by others as well as the uncontrollable urge to extend it

Appreciate the above: You will find yourself slowing down and living in that quiet inner space where you can appreciate what come your way. You will know in your heart that you need not be threatened by the views or actions of anyone else. You will receive more joy and ease in your life, because that is what you will be sending out. You will find it easier to accept contrary views, knowing that you are not defined by anything or anyone external to yourself.

Dr. Wayne W. Dyer

In a world of individuals, comparison makes no sense at all.

Dr. Wayne W. Dyer

Men grow alike if they breathe the same air and share the same atmosphere. Nature abhors these complaisance's, which threaten to melt the world into a lump.

Emerson

Heaven reserves an equal scope for all of us. Each person is uneasy until he has produced his private ray and has seen his talent at his highest with pride and elation.

Emerson

If we can articulate who we are, then we have learned to express our individuality. Aristotle said, "Men acquire a particular quality by constantly acting in a particular way.

Each individual is the child of his or her peers at a definite stage of development. Only through his own effort can an individual begin harmony with his own substance. He or she must bring the will demanded by his own peers to his own consciousness, to clear expression of what he is. the individual does not invent his own content; he is what he is only by acting out what he is. Realness, truth, honesty takes over where nothing else will.

"You are the first you, that ever was."

Thoreau's most influential essay, "Civil disobedience," helped him become the American prophet of individualism. The spirit of independence became a way of life for him.

Those who claim nothing of them selves have nothing to give. Most people have more to give than they realize.

Jacques Barzan

The ultimate goal of the education system is to shift to the individual the burden of pursuing his own education.

John W.Gardner

Only a few people at any time in human history have enjoyed the challenge of "making" themselves; most have fled from the unendurable burden of freedom into the womblike security of the group. The new age of social mobility may be fine for those strong enough to discover and develop their own roles, but for the timid and the frightened, who constitute the majority in any age, the vacant spaces of equalitarian society can become a nightmare.

Arthur M. Schlesinger, Jr.

A man of learning is a man who has learned a great deal; a man of genius, one from who we learn something, which the genius has learned from nobody.

Schopenhauer

If a man has a talent and cannot use it, he has failed. If he has a talent and uses only half of it, he has partly failed. If he has a talent and learns somehow to use the whole of it, he has gloriously succeeded, and won a satisfaction and a triumph few men ever know

Thomas Wolfe

The credit belongs to the man who is actually in the arena; whose face is marred by dust and sweat and blood; who strives valiantly; who errs and comes short again and again; who knows the great enthusiasms, the great devotions, and spends himself in a worth cause; who at the best knows in the end the triumph of high achievement; and who at the worst, if he fails, at least fails while daring greatly.

Theodore Roosevelt

He who has done his best for his own time has lived for all times.

Johann Von Schiller

If there's a way to do it better find it.

Thomas A. Edison

To be what we are, and to become what we are capable of becoming, is the only end of life.

Robert Louis Stevenson

At has become an individual statement and, for the artist himself, a means whereby he can pursue his own self-realization.

Anthony Storrs

The creative person is constantly seeking to discover himself, to remodel his own identity, and to find meaning in the universe through what he creates. He finds this a valuable integrating process which, like meditation or prayer, has little to do with other people, but which has its own separate validity. His most significant moments are those in which he attains some new insight, or makes some new discovery; and these moments are chiefly, if not invariably, those in which he is alone.

Anthony Storrs

A man's dreams are an index to his greatness.

Zadok Rabinowitz

"Cease to be ruled by dogmas and authorities; look at the world."

Roger Bacon

Far away there in the sunshine are my highest aspirations. I may not reach them, but I can look up and see their beauty, believe in them, and try to follow where they lead.

Louisa May Alcott

There isn't any particular way that life is to be lived, life is to precious and brief to be excessively governed by what other people might think.

Keith Johnsgard, Ph. D.

Fifty Plus Runners Assoc.

It is hard to have a sense of responsibility if one feels wholly powerless and unconnected to events.

John W.Gardner

(The above statement is part of the reason excellence is not a way of thinking for young students. They must do what (they) are told, rather than follow their own energy and enthusiasm.)

He is great who is what he is from nature and who never reminds us of others.

Emerson

The river makes its own shores, and each legitimate idea makes its own channels.

Everson

Man is endogenous, and education is his unfolding, The aid we have from others is mechanical, compared with the discoveries of nature in us...what is thus learned is delightful in the doing, and the effect remains.

Emerson

What count's in any system is the intelligence, self-control, conscience and energy of the individual.

Cyrus Eaton.

Regardless of circumstances, each man lives in a world of his own making.

Josepha Murray Emms.

No task is so humble that it does not offer an outlet in individuality.

William Feather.

Every individual has a place to fill in the world, and is important in some respect, whether he chooses to be so or not.

Nathaniel Hawthorne.

It is an absolute perfection to know how to get the very most out of one's individuality.

Michel De Montaigne.

Individuality is everywhere to be spaced and respected as the root of everything good.

Jean Paul Richter.

It is said that if Noah's ark had had to be built by a company, they would not have laid the keel yet; and it may be so. What is many men's business is nobody's business. The greatest things are accomplished by individual men.

Charles H. Spurgeon.

One man can completely change the character of a country, and the industry of its people, by dropping a single seed in fertile soil.

John C. Gifford.

The American system is of rugged individualism.

Herbert Clark Hoover.

The common phrase, "building a personality" is a misnomer. Personality is not so much like a structure as like a river, it continuously flows, and to be a person is to be engaged in a perpetual process of becoming.

Harry Emerson Fosdick.

The worth of a state, in the long run, is the worth of the individuals composing it.

John Stuart Mill.

Whoso would be a man, must be a Nonconformist.

Emerson.

I think we should be men first, and subjects afterward.

Henry David Thoreau.

KNOWLEDGE

The only good is knowledge and the only evil is ignorance.
Socrates

Men love to wonder, and that is the seed of science.
Emerson

Knowledge is only potential power. It becomes power only
when, and if, it is organized into definite plans of action and
directed to a definite end. The missing link in all systems of
education may be found in the failure of educational institutions
to teach their students how to organize and use knowledge after
they acquire it.
Napoleon Hill

The average young person is quick to make sweeping,
positive statements, but the man who has lived long in the world
usually speaks with caution when making specific declarations.
Knowledge makes man humble. True genius is always modest. It
has been so down through the ages. The greatest and wisest were
also the meekest and humblest.
John D. Snider

One of the sublime rewards of reading a brilliant writer is
to catch his penetrating flashes that cast light into dark corners,
illumine dim by-paths, and point the way to realms of gold where
the mind finds knowledge and the spirit of refreshment.
John D. Snider

If you have knowledge, let others light their candles at it.
Margaret Fuller

Knowledge is a comfortable and necessary retreat and shelter
for us in an advanced age; and if we do not plant it while young, it
will give us no shade when we grow old.
Lord Chesterfield

Sciences may be learned by rote, but wisdom not.
Laurence Sterne

The judge should not be young; he should have learned to know evil, not from his own soul, but from late and long observation of the nature of evil in others: Knowledge should be his guide, not personal experience.
Plato

The desire of knowledge, like the thirst of riches, increases ever with the acquisition of it.
Laurence Sterne

The desire of possessor in excess caused man to fall.
Bacon

Knowledge is power.
Bacon

Consider your origin; ye were not formed to live like brutes, but to follow virtue and knowledge.
Dante

Where there is much desire to learn, there of necessity will be much arguing, much writing, many opinions; for opinion in good men is but knowledge in the making.
Milton

In much wisdom is much grief: and he that increaseth knowledge increaseth sorrow.
Proverbs. XXXI

Knowledge is of two kinds: we know a subject ourselves, or we know where we can find information upon it.
Samuel Johnson

Knowledge is proud that he has learned so much;
Wisdom is humble that he knows no more.
William Cowper

Knowledge, in truth, is the great sun in the firmament. Life and power are scattered with all its beams.

Webster

In learning a new language a man has, as it were, to mark out in his mind the boundaries of quite new spheres of ideas, with the result that spheres of ideas arise where none were before. Thus he not only learns words, be gains ideas too.

Schopenhauer

The richest soil, if uncultivated, produces the rankest weeds.

Plutarch

Man's mind, once stretched by a new idea, never regains its original dimensions.

Oliver Wendell Holmes

If you accomplish anything in this world, it will be because you have power. Knowledge is power. Our literature from Chaucer to Eliot contains enough to make a man happy, thoughtful, and eloquent through an entire lifetime.

Gilbert Highet

The young men of this land are not, as they are often called, a "lost" race-they are a race that never yet has been discovered. And the whole secret, power, and knowledge of their own discovery is locked within them-and they cannot utter it.

Thomas Wolfe

He said that there was one only good, namely, knowledge; and one only evil, namely, ignorance.

Diogenes Laertius

Bodily exercise, when compulsory, does no harm to the body, but knowledge which is acquired under compulsion obtains no hold on the mind.

Plato

In practical matter the end is not mere speculative knowledge of what is to be done, but rather the doing of it. It is not enough to know about Virtue, then, but we must endeavour to possess it, and to use it, or to take any other steps that may make us good.

Aristotle

The only fence against the world is a thorough knowledge of it.

John Locke

The great end of life is not knowledge but action.
Thomas Henry Hawley

Love is ever the beginning of knowledge, as fire is of light.
Thomas Carlyle

A wise man is strong; yea, a man of knowledge increaseth strength.

Proverb XXII. 31

The knowledge of the world is only to be acquired in the world, not in a closet.

Chesterfield

> The tissue of the life to be
> We weave with colors all our own,
> And in the field of Destiny
> We reap as we have sown.
> Whittier

I think that a knowledge of Greek thought and life, and of the arts in which the Greeks expressed their thought and sentiment, essential to high culture. A man may know everything else, but without this knowledge he remains ignorant of the best intellectual and moral achievements of his own race.

Charles Eliot Norton

> Men are polished, through act and speech,
> Each by each,
> As pebbles are smoothed on the
> rolling beach.
> With years a richer life begins,
> The spirit mellows:
> Ripe age gives tone to violins,
> Wine, and good fellow.

John Townsend Trowbridge

Only on the edge of the grave can man conclude anything.

Henry Brooks Adams

A man ought to read just as inclination leads him; for what he reads as a task will do him little good. A young man should read five hours in a day and so may acquire a great deal of knowledge.

Samuel Johnson

The book which you read from a sense of duty, or because for any reason you must, does not commonly make friends with you.

William Dean Howells

The judge should not be young; he should have learned to know evil not from his own soul, but from late and long observation of the nature of evil in others; knowledge should be his guide, not personal experience.

Plato

No man's knowledge here can go beyond his experience.

John Locke

In spite of difference of soil and climate, of language and manner, of laws and custom-in spite of things silently gone out of mind, and things violently destroyed, the Poet binds together by passion and knowledge the vast empire of human society, as it is spread over the whole earth, and over all time.
Wordsworth

As the Spanish proverb says, "he, who would bring home the wealth of the Indies, must carry the wealth of the Indies with him," so it is in traveling, man must carry knowledge with him if he would bring home knowledge.
Samuel Johnson

That there should one-man die ignorant who had capacity for knowledge, this I call a tragedy.
Thomas Carlyle

Knowledge comes, but wisdom lingers.
Tennyson

From contemplation one may become wise, but knowledge comes only from study.
A.Edward Newton

If you have knowledge, let others light their candles at it.
Thomas Fuller.

It is knowledge that ultimately gives salvation.
Gandhi.

Knowledge of our duties is the most essential part of the philosophy of life. If you escape duty you avoid action. The world demands results.
George Washington Goethals.

The seeds of knowledge may be planted in solitude, but must be cultivated in public.

Samuel Johnson.

I keep six honest serving-men
(They taught me all I knew);
Their names are What and Why and When
And How and Where and Who.

Rudyard Kipling.

A taste of every sort of knowledge is necessary to form the mind.

John Locke.

The desire of knowledge, like the thirst of riches, increases ever with the acquisition of it.

Laurence Sterne.

The end of all knowledge should be in virtuous action.

Sir Philip Sidney.

The wise man realizes how little he knows: it is the foolish person who imagines that he knows everything.

Jawaharlal Nehru.

The word knowledge, strictly employed, implies three things: truth, proof, and conviction.

Richard Whatley.

KNOW-THYSELF

If we know ourselves well enough, we know that our real capacity far exceeds the average expectations others have for us.

Harvey Mackay

No one-can teach you how to be yourself.
Warren Bennis

It is far more important to understand yourself, the constant changing of the facts about yourself, than to meditate in order to find God, have visions, sensations and other forms of entertainment.
J. Krishnamurti
Krishnamurti 's Notebook p.177

They can conquer who believe they can. It is he who has done the deed once who does not shrink from attempting it again.
Everson

They can do all because they think they can.
Virgil

Men must be decided on what they will not do, and then they are able to act with vigor in what they ought to do.
Mencius

All men by nature desire to know.
Aristotle

When we cannot find contentment in ourselves it is useless to seek it elsewhere.
Francois de La Rochefaucauld

A man can know nothing of mankind without knowing something of himself. Self-knowledge is the property of that man whose passions have their full play, yet who ponders over their results.
Disraeli

He who know others is worldly, but he who also knows himself is wise.
Ancient proverb

A world stretched out before me,
dimly seen, by just the set sun,
Lord, show me my task, my talent,
my share in the great undone.
    Stella Grace Julian.

The delights of self-discovery are always available.
Gail Sheehy.

If you have your language and you have your culture, and
you're not ashamed of it, then you know who you are.
    Maria Urquides.

CHAPTER 11

QUOTATIONS

LEADERSHIP

Who cannot rule himself, how should he rule others?
Confucius

Most leaders suffer from what I call "controlitis." They feel more secure when all the butterflies are flying in formation. If someone makes waves they feel insecure.   Risk, not security is the proving grounds of progress, growth, and improvement. If you don't have the courage to be different you become just another, "also-ran." You and your institution become like everything else, either mediocre or worse. You don't challenge people, when you control them. You don't inspire people, when you control them. Everything in this world and every person has a natural bent. We all have a tendency to do what interests us most. Your responsibility is to educate those you lead, as individuals. Individualism needs inspired leadership. A manager's responsibility is to bring out the best in people. Excellence cannot be created if all of your time is focused on the word "control."
R. V. E.

Authority has an invisible weakness, because it boasts truth without being effective. It claims to win because of top position, rather than listening to the thoughts of others. It is machoism in disguise.

R. V. E.

Not all readers
are necessarily leaders.
but all leaders
are readers.

Our chief want in life is somebody who shall make us do what we can.

Emerson

All great leaders know the value of timing, creative insight, sensitivity, vision, versatility, and focus. All play a role in success stories.

Do not go where the path may lead, go where there is no path and leave a trail.

Leadership must look at chaos, complexity, perplexity in a way that says, "We are going to struggle with this." Molders of opinion, those who profess leadership abilities are hiding in a forest of trees unnecessarily. Their modesty hides a distinction only they have.

Jacques Barzun

Successful leaders are not authoritarian; but educators, motivators, adult changers.

The remaining frontier: successful channeling of human talent and energy into constructive outlets.

The power leaders communicate is not theirs.

Become a leader not a greeter.

Leadership doesn't mean having all the answers. It means asking the right questions. You demonstrate your confidence in your people by giving them freedom to do the job you hired them to do. Be like Jockey Willie Shoemaker. He's the best in the business because he has the lightest touch on the reins. They say the horse never knows he's there-unless he's needed.

Harvey Mackay

On the wall of your mind should hang a vision of what you ought to be and can be. Dreamers are not surprised by success when it comes; because they have seen it coming, and planned out it's coming, in their dreams. The really valuable work of the day could have been and should have been done under the shower in the morning, or in the fifteen minute walk across the park to the office. It is easy to become so engrossed with the mere mechanics of business as to lose the habit of thought. Success is the maximum utilization of the ability that you have

Zig Ziglar

The kind of people I look for to fill top management spots are the eager beaver, the mavericks. These are the guys who try to do more than they're expected to do; they always reach.

Lee Iacocca

As I grow older, I pay less attention to what men say. I just watch what they do.

Andrew Carnegie.

The people who get on in this world are the people who get up and look for the circumstances they want, and, if they can't find them, make them.

George Bernard Shaw

When you hire people who are smarter than you, you are proving you are smarter than they are.
R. H. Grant

There is something that is much more scarce, something rarer than ability. It is the ability to recognize ability.
Robert Half

It is one of the most beautiful compensations of this life that no man can sincerely try to help another without helping himself.
Ralph Waldo Emerson

The speed of the leader determines the rate of the pack. There isn't any particular way that life is to be lived and that life is to precious and brief to be excessively governed by what other people might think.
Keith Johnsgard, Ph. D.
Fifty-Plus Runners Assoc.

If any man could discover a means of judging and choosing correctly and rationally, he would, by that act alone establish a perfect form of government.
Montaigne

In those high places common sense is rarely to be found.
Juvenal

It is a peculiar kind of instinct, which drives the man of genius to give permanent form to what he sees and feels wit.
Schopenhauer

Like the ordinary man, the genius is what he is chiefly for himself. This is essential to his nature: a fact, which can neither be avoiced nor altered.
Schopenhauer

Leadership and learning are indispensable to each other.
John Fitzgerald Kennedy.

Leadership is the other side of the coin of loneliness, and he who is a leader must always act alone. And acting alone, accept everything alone.
Ferdinand Marcos.

Blindness in a leader is unpardonable.
Jawaharlal Nehru.

The leader must know, must know that he knows, and must be able to make it abundantly clear to those about him that he knows.
Clarence Belden Randall.

A leader is a dealer in hope.
Napoleon Bonaparte.

A man who wants to lead the orchestra must turn his back on the crowd.
James Crook.

You do not lead by hitting people over the head--that's assault, not leadership.
Dwight D. Eisenhower.

It's often a good idea to let the other fellow believe he is running things whether he is or not.
William Feather.

Real leaders are ordinary people with extraordinary determinations.
John Seaman Garns.

A great leader never sets himself above his followers except in carrying responsibilities.
Jules Ormont.

The best leaders are those most interested in surrounding themselves with assistants and associates smarter than they are—being frank in admitting this--and willing to pay for such talents.
Amos Parrish.

Leaders do not understand that Civil Service examinations can not grade men in loyalty, vision, integrity, teamwork, and tenacity, which rate even higher than native ability as qualifications for industrial leadership.
Edgar M. Queeny

You will never be a leader unless you first learn to follow and be led.
Tiorio.

Leadership is the ability to get men to do what they don't want to do and like it.
Harry S. Truman.

It is hard to look up to a leader who keeps his ear to the ground.
James H. Boren.

I must follow the people. Am I not their leader?
Benjamin Disraeli.

Today a reader; tomorrow a leader.
W. Fusselman.

If you command wisely, you'll be obeyed cheerfully.
Thomas Fuller.

No one's a leader if there are no followers.
Malcolm Forbes.

Those who can command themselves command others.
William Hazlitt.

Leadership is action, not position.
Donald H. McGannon.

The crux of leadership is that you must constantly stop to consider how your decisions will influence people.
Michigan State Police Maxim.

A great leader never sets himself above his followers except in carrying responsibilities.
Jules Ormont.

Reason and judgment are the qualities of a leader.
Tacitus.

Leadership is the ability to get men to do what they don't want to do and like it.
Harry S. Truman.

Produce great men, the rest follows
Walt Whitman

The best leaders are those most interested in surrounding themselves with assistants and associates smarter than they are-being, frank in admitting this-and willing to pay for such talents.
Amos Parrish

A good leader inspires men to have confidence in him; a great leader inspires them to have confidence in themselves.

LIFE

ANYWAY

People are unreasonable, illogical and self-centered.
Love them anyway.
If you do good people will accuse you of selfish ulterior
motives.
Do good anyway.
If you are successful, you will win false friends and true
enemies.
      Succeed anyway.
   Honesty and frankness make you vulnerable.
      Be honest and frank anyway.
The good you do today will be forgotten tomorrow.
      Do good anyway.
The biggest people with the biggest ideas can be shot down by
the smallest people with the smallest minds.
      Think big anyway.
  People favor underdogs but follow only top dogs.
      Fight for some underdogs anyway.
What you spend years building may be destroyed overnight.
      Build anyway.
Give the world the best you have and you'll get kicked in the
teeth.
      Give the world the best you've got anyway.
Quoted in Response and
1982 Readers Digest p.248

A wise man will make more opportunities than he finds.
Francis Bacon

Mankind is in itself not at all inclined to award praise and
reputation; it is more disposed to blame and find fault, whereby it
indirectly praises itself.
Schopenhauer.

Problems are only opportunities in work clothes.
Henry J. Kaiser

He who wishes to experience gratitude from his contemporaries, must adjust his pace to theirs. But great things are never produced in this way.
Schopenhauer

1) What are the limits of human faculty in various directions?

2) By what diversity of means, in the differing types of human beings, may the faculties be stimulated to their best results?

As a rule men habitually use only a small part of the powers which they actually possess and which they might use under appropriate conditions. Stating the thing broadly, the human individual thus lives usually far within his limit: he losses powers of various sorts, which he habitually fails to use. He energized below his maximum and he behaves below his optimum. Excitement, ideas, and efforts, in a word, are what carry us over the dam to leadership.

We find that the stimuli that carry us over the usually effective dam are most often the classic emotional ones, love, anger, crow-contagion, or despair. Despair lames most people, but it wakes others fully up. We are all to some degree oppressed, un-free. We don't come to our own, it is there, but we don 't get at it. The threshold must be made to shift. Then many of us find the eccentric activity-a "spree," say-relieves. There is no doubt that to some men sprees and excesses of almost any kind are medicinal, temporally at any rate, in spite of what the moralists and doctors say. But when the normal tasks and stimulation of life don't put a man's deeper levels of energy on tap, and requires distinctly deleterious excitements, his constitution verges on the abnormal.

The normal opener of deeper and deeper levels of energy is the will.
William James
The Practical Cogitator p. 120

The vocation of every man and women is to serve other people.
Tolstoi

To be what we are, and to become what we are capable of becoming, is the only end of life.
Robert Louis Stevenson

Life is not only work, but is also play and suffering, beauty and pain, joy and sorrow, sunshine and rain, disgrace and glory, darkness, storm and terror, as well as sweetness, peace and light.
Albert E. Wiggan

Society is organized for profit instead of for happiness.
Albert E. Wiggan

I need to know people who are alive.
Anais Nin

I want the utmost that anyone can offer me, and in return I will give the utmost.
Henry Miller

Live your life each day, as you would climb a mountain. An occasional glance toward the summit keeps the goal in mind, but many beautiful scenes are to be observed from each new vantage point. Climb slowly, steadily; enjoying each passing moment; and the view from the summit will serve as a fitting climax for the journey.
Harold V. Melchert

Life is like riding a bicycle. You don't fall off unless you stop pedaling.
Claude Pepper

The wisdom of life consists of eliminating the non-essentials, and of finding contentment in those things closest to us.
Samuel Johnson

The men who succeed best in public life are those who take the risk of standing by their own convictions.
James A. Garfield

As soon as there is life there is danger.
Ralph Waldo Emerson

Live dangerously and you live right.
Goethe

Death is not the greatest loss in life. The greatest loss is what dies inside us while we live.
Norman Cousins

He fills his lifetime with deeds, not with inactive years.
Ovid

Who never doubted never half believed?
Philip James Bailey

Go confidently in the direction of your dreams! Live the life you've imagined! As you simplify your life, the laws of the universe will be simpler, solitude will not be solitude, poverty will not be poverty, nor weakness, weakness.
Henry David Thoreau

So to conduct one's life as to realize oneself this seems to me the highest attainment possible to a human being. It is the task of one and all of us, but most of us bungle it.

Henrik Ibsen

If a man does not make new acquaintances, as he advances through life he will soon find himself left alone. A man, Sir, should keep his friendships in constant repair.

Samuel Johnson

All human actions have one or more of these causes: chance, nature, compulsion, habit, reason, passion, desire.

Aristotle

Everywhere in life, the true question is not what we gain, but what we do.

Thomas Carlyle

Life does not consist of thinking it consists in acting.

Woodrow Wilson

It is better to wear out than to rust out.

Bishop Cumberland

Be not afraid of life. Believe that life is worth living and your belief will help create the fact.

William James

The utmost we can hope for in this world is contentment; if we aim at anything higher, we shall meet with nothing but grief and disappointment.

Joseph Addison

Of the blessings set before you, make your choice and be content.

Samuel Johnson

One hour of life, crowded to the full with glorious action, and filled with noble risks, is worth whole years of those mean observances of paltry decorum, in which men steal through existence, like sluggish waters through a marsh, without either honour or observation.
Sir Waiter Scott

The quality of a person's life is in direct proportion to their commitment to excellence, regardless of their chosen field of endeavor.
Vincent T. Lombardi

Why am I here? To find out what happens next!!!
Television interview
Two men sailing around
the world...

LISTENING

There is no greater loan than a sympathetic ear.
Many receive advice, only the wise profit.
Syrus.

Ignore what a man desires and you ignore the very source of his power.
Waiter Lippman.

Listen behind the humor and politeness...listen, for a change, to what isn't being said. Instead of ignoring the tension in a conversation, pay attention to it. Try to understand the disagreement that isn't quite being expressed, and how it might affect the outcome of the discussion or conversation.
Alien F Harrison and Robert
M. Bramson. Ph. D.
Styles of Thinking.

I went to something called "Active Listening" in active listening you rephrase what everyone says, which means that you distort everything they say. Then we began to pay attention to what really divergent people who were "wizards" actually do.

Richard Bandler and John Grinder.
Frogs into Princes.

Goethe, faithful to his rule of getting the best out of every situation, preferred to listen. Somewhere I read that two people would rather go to bed with each other than they would express to each other exactly what they feel and think. Buber believed people should carry on important dialogue with each other. We must heed, affirm and confirm the existence of each other.

Norman Cousins

Don't waste time arguing and contradicting, look to learn; try to find the other fellow as he's known to himself. Try to find out what he thinks of himself.

Benjamin DeMott
Supergrow p.167

Silence is one great art of conversation. He is not a fool who knows when to hold his tongue.

William Hazlitt.

No one is so savage that he cannot become civilized, if he will lend a patient ear to culture.

Horace

One does not have to believe everything one hears.
Cicero

Go somewhere you can be totally alone; a place where no one is looking at you or expecting anything from you. Have a pencil in hand and paper to write on. Now listen to yourself. Write one word in the upper right hand corner that describes what you are thinking about. Expect to write fast; be totally honest with yourself. You may, at a later time, want to destroy or expand on what you have written, but for now, respect your thinking with paper and pen. You will be surprised with the variety and depth of your thinking. You have knowledge and wisdom you are not aware of. You can win more friends with your ears than with your mouth.

CHAPTER 12

QUOTATIONS

LOVE

The best portion of a good man's life-his little nameless, unremembered acts of kindness and of love.
William Wordsworth

Life without love is like a tree without blossom and fruit.
Kahill Gibran.

We are all born for love. It is the principle of existence, and it's only end.
Benjamin Disraeli

He has achieved success who has lived well, laughed often, and loved much.
Anonymous

The moment you have in your heart this extra ordinary thing called love and feel the depth, the delight , the ecstasy of it, you will discover that for you the world is transformed.
J. Krishnamurti

Life in abundance comes only through great love.
Elbert Hubbard

What force is more potent than love?
Igor Stravinsky

Finding oneself' is not something one does alone. The quest for personal growth and self-fulfillment is supposed to lead one into relationships with others, and most important among them are love and marriage.
Habits of the heart. p. 85

We find ourselves not independently of other people and institutions, but through them. We never get to the bottom of our selves on our own. We discover who we are face to face and side by side with others in work, love, and learning.
Habit of the Heart   P. 85

To love someone means to see him as God intended him.
Dostovevsky

If I am vulnerable, there is no need for me to pretend.
Anonymous

Tis better to have loved and lost, than never to have loved at all.
Tennyson

So long as we love we serve, so long as we are indispensable, and no man is useless while he has a friend.
Stevenson

A man who dominates is a man who does not love. He has a tremendous animal vitality, a force, which conquers. He conquers, people are subjected to him, but he neither loves nor understands.

He is just a force and he is filled with his own strength. If he loves at all, it is a force like his own, and so again he loves his own kind of strength, not the other, which is an infiltration. Watch the conqueror well, watch the man or women who dominates another: he is not the one who loves. The one who loves is the one who is dominated. You love me, and so you cannot dominate me, and I being a woman sought domination.

Anais Nin.

Do all things with love.
Og Mandino

I want the utmost that anyone can offer me, and in return I will give the utmost.
Henry Miller

Treasure the love you receive above all. It will survive long after your gold and good healths have vanished.
Og Mandino

Love is life...and if you miss love, you miss life.
Leo Buscaglia

Where there is love there is life.
Mohandas Gandhi

You will find as you look back upon your life that the moments when you have really lived, are the moments when you have really lived, are the moments when you have done things in a spirit of love.
Henry Drummond

Of all earthly music, that which reaches farthest into Heaven is the beating of a truly loving heart.
Henry Ward Beecher.

It is as absurd to say that a man can't love one woman all the time as it is to say that a violinist needs several violins to play the same piece of music.
Honore De Balzac.

Of all discriminations-
Decry them as you will-
The ultimate is love:
Forever or until?
Art Buck.

We should measure affection, not like youngsters by the ardor of its passions, but by its strength and constancy.
Cicero

To live without loving is not really to live
Moliere.

Everywhere, we learn only from those whom we love.
Goethe.

We are shaped and fashioned by what we love.
Goethe.

Love is what's left of a relationship after all the selfishness has been removed.
Cullen Hightower.

MISTAKES

MISTAKES ARE THE SOURCE OF ALL GREAT LEARNING.

Even mistakes may turn out to be the thing necessary to a worthwhile achievement.
Henry Ford

He knows not his own strength that hath not met adversity.
Ben Jonson

Two things a man should never be angry at: what he can help,
and what he cannot help.
Thomas Fuller

The man who trusts men will make fewer mistakes than he
who distrusts them.
Cavour

The greater the difficulty, the greater the glory.
Cicero

Settle one difficulty and you keep a hundred others away.
Ancient proverb

It gives me great pleasure to converse with the aged. They
have been over the road that all of us must travel, and know where
it is rough and difficult and where it is level and easy.
Plato

Courage and perseverance have a magical talisman, before
which difficulties disappear and obstacles vanish into air.
John Quincy Adams

Love the truth but pardon error.
Voltaire

The freedom to fail is vital if you're going to succeed. Most
successful men fail time and time again, and it is a measure of
their strength that failure merely propels them into some new
attempt at success.
Michael Korda

Failure is only the opportunity to more intelligently begin again.
Henry Ford

The greatest mistake a man can make is to be afraid of making one.
Elbert Hubbard

Failure is success if we learn from it.
Malcolm S. Forbes

Don't be afraid to fail. Don't waste energy trying to cover up failure. Learn from your failures and go on to the next challenge. It's OK to fail. If you're not failing, you're not growing.
H. Stanley Judd

In some attempts, it is glorious even to fail.
Longinus.

The difference between greatness and mediocrity is often how an individual views a mistake.
Nelson Boswell

The successful man will profit from his mistakes and try again in a different way.
Dale Carnegie

No man ever achieved worthwhile success who did not, at one time or other; find himself with at least one foot hanging well over the brink of failure.
Napoleon Hill

Opportunity often comes disguised in the form of misfortune, or temporary defeat.
Napoleon Hill

Success seems to be connected with action. Successful men keep moving. They make mistakes, but they don't quit.
Conrad Hilton

The majority of men meet with failure because of their lack of persistence in creating new plans to take the place of those, which fail.
Napoleon Hill

More people would learn from their mistakes if they weren't so busy denying that they made them.
Anonymous.

Wise men learn by other men's mistakes, fools by their own.
H.G. Brown.

Life is very interesting, if you make mistakes.
Georges Carpentier.

A man who has committed a mistake and doesn't correct it is committing another mistake.
Confucius.

He who makes no mistakes, never makes anything.
English Proverb.

The greatest mistake you can make in life is to be continually fearing you will make one.
Elbert Hubbard.

Men must try and try again. They must suffer the consequences of their own mistakes and learn by their own failures and their own successes.
Lawson Purdy.

He who never made a mistake never made a discovery.
Samuel Smiles.

I don't care what people say about me. I do care about my mistakes.
Socrates.

Learn from the mistakes of others--you can't live long enough to make them all yourself.
Martin Vanbee.

Experience is simply the name we give our mistakes.
Oscar Wilde.

OPTIMISM

The cynic is one who never sees a good quality in a man, and never fails to see and bad one. He is the human owl, vigilant in darkness, and blind to light, musing for vermin, and never seeing noble game.
Henry Ward Beecher

I hate cynicism a great deal worse than I do the devil; unless perhaps, the two were the same thing?
Robert Louis Stevenson

He who fears being conquered is sure of defeat.
Napoleon Bonaparte

The true worth of a man is to be measure by the objects he pursues,
Marcus Aurelius

Every man who can be a first-rate something-as every man can be who is a man at all-has no right to be a fifth-rate something; for a fifth something is no better than a first- rate nothing.
J.G. Holland

Hope is itself a species of happiness, and, perhaps, the chief happiness which this world affords.
Samuel Johnson

The grand essentials to happiness in this life are something to do, something to love, and something to hope for.
Joseph Addison

A mind always employed is always happy. This is the true secret, the grand recipe, for felicity.
Thomas Jefferson

To be happy, memorize something good each day, see something beautiful each day, do something helpful each day.
Ancient proverb

He who is of a calm and happy nature will hardly feel the pressure of age, but to him who is of an opposite disposition, youth and age are equally a burden.
Plato

The future belongs to those who believe in the beauty of their dreams.
Eleanor Roosevelt

All things are difficult before they are easy.
John Norley

Small opportunities are often the beginning of great enterprises.
Demosthenes

To travel hopefully is a better thing than to arrive.
Stevenson

Remember the steam kettle! Though up to its neck in hot water, it continues to sing.

In the middle of difficulty lies opportunity
Albert Einstein

It's the constant and determined effort that breaks down all resistance, sweeps away all obstacles.
Claude M. Brisiol

Destiny is not a matter of chance; it is a matter of choice.

The future shouldn't be a disaster. It should be an opportunity.
Urquhart

A pessimist tries to figure out what is wrong; they see the speck on the window instead of the sunset.
Anonymous

The ideal man bears the accidents of life with dignity and grace, making the best of circumstances.
Aristotle

They dared beyond their strength, hazarded beyond their judgment and in extremities were of excellent hope.
Thucydides

Unless a man undertakes more than he possibly can do, he will never do all he can do.
Henry Drummond

The chiefest action for a man of spirit is never to be out of action; the soul was never put in the body to stand still.
John Webster

In adversity a man is saved by hope.
Menander

If you count the sunny and cloudy day through a year, you will find that sunshine predominates
Ovid

Are you in earnest? Seize this very minute; What you can do, or dream you can, begin it; Boldness has genius, power and magic in it. Only engage and the mind grows heated; begin and then the work will be completed.
Goethe

It is not the brains that matter most, but that which guides them--character, the heart, generous qualities, progressive ideas.
Dostoevsky

The man who trusts men will make fewer mistakes than he who distrusts them.
Cavour

One of the things I learned the hard way was that it doesn't pay to get discouraged. Keeping busy and making optimism a way of life can restore your faith in yourself.
Lucile Ball

PARENTING

As far as I know, excluding myself, there is no such thing as a perfect parent. All parents make mistakes, but there is a recovery for every situation. LOVE, true honest, sincere love covers most mistakes we make. Love should be given every possible chance to shine through.

Parents are just learning to be parents and children are learning to be children. Both can be considered in the amateur status group. Hopefully, they are learning and growing. Parents, however because of their physical size can dominate what often appears to be a competitive situation.

They can and do become the authority figure. They often use their size, which becomes official status, like the position of a high officer in a large company. Their size or position often becomes intimidation which is wrongful use of power. If fairness is important to you, it could be said, "authority can be unfair."

A child and parent are both human beings working side by side with the same purpose and goals. They are a two-man team working towards humanness and fulfillment of their purpose in life; whatever that may be. Everyone has their own God given talent and ability. Each will eventually find their way in life. Since they are together in the same household they may as well help each other find or fulfill their own destiny. That destiny is to find and use all that has been given them.

A parents purpose at this time, is to help the younger generation learn all they can learn about themselves, it's part of growing up. So the relationship between parent and child should be considered, equally, nothing more than the interaction of two human beings. I think true love makes respect for each other necessary. When your children become adults, you will realize how little difference there is between you and your child

Learning suggestion:
Write, with total honesty, what kind
of relationship you should have with
your parents. You will find the need
to improve your essay several times.
You will change, and so will your parents.

Parents often give the impression, that having a child shows ownership. Not true. Neither parent nor child has more rights or privileges then the other. Both owe each other respect, the same they would expect for themselves. Neither is the "boss," it's a democracy. We are both in the same-boat in this sea of life and destiny, what ever it happens to be.

Children test their parents. That's the way it should be, unless they have been told they are to be "seen and not heard." Parents test themselves in society. This is as it should be, unless they have allowed society beat them down; into meekness, or submission.

Both children and parents lose their fighting spirit easily. Like rolling stones, I shape you and shape me, we shape each other, and are shaped; sometimes into conformity. Authority is often abusive, without realizing what it has done.

A parent is nobody special because of who they are. A parent is an individual very much like the individual their child is. The chance of two people being exactly the same are trillions and trillions to one; so, respect for each others individuality is not even debatable.

When you give respect to a "little one" you are using an effective teaching tool. It gives the learner confidence; a good feeling about themselves. All ages of people react in a positive way to respect. We all try to live up to the respect that has been given us. So, what I'm trying to say briefly is, create an atmosphere where little people are encouraged to make mistakes, and be responsible for their mistakes. This gives them an opportunity to discover on their own a better way when they try again. Strong children, very much like when they are learning to walk, do not hesitate, when it's time to try again.

They must keep on taking risks all of their lives, so now is the time to develop the risk taking habit.

Do not read books on parenting, read books on leadership. You are, like it or not, a leader.
R.V.E.

Parenthood remains the greatest single preserve of the amateur.
Alvin Toffler

Our aim is to discipline children for activity, for work, for good; not for immobility, passivity, obedience.
Maria Montiessori

You can do anything with children if you only play with them.
Prince Otto Von Bismarck

By the year 2000 we will, I hope, raise our children to believe in human potential.
Gloria Steinem

If a child lives with approval, he learns to live with himself.
Dorothy Law Nolte

A three-year old child is a being who gets almost as much fun out of a fifty-six dollar set of swings as it does out of finding a small green worm.
Bill Vaughan

If you want to see what children can do, you must stop giving them things.
Norman Douglas

Too often we give children answers to remember rather than problems to solve.

Roger Lewin

The fault no child ever loses is the one he was most pushed for.

Cesare Beccaria

Likely as not, the child you can do the least with will do the most to make you proud.

Mignon McLaughlin

To bring up a child in the way he should go, travel that way yourself once in a while.

Josh Billings.

We try to make our children become more like us, instead of trying to become more like them--with the result that we pick up none of their good traits, and they pick up most of our bad ones.

Sydney J. Harris.

Adolescence is the period of life when we first become obsessed with trying to prove we are not a child--an obsession that can last a lifetime.

Cullen Hightower.

Pretty much, all the honest truth telling there is in the world is done by children.

Oliver Wendell Holmes.

CHAPTER 13

QUOTATIONS

READING

A man should not read to much, in order that his mind may not become accustomed to the substitute and thereby forget the reality; that it may not form the habit of walking in well-worn paths; nor by following an alien course of thought grow a stranger to its own. The real life that a man sees before him is the natural subject of thought; and in its strength as the primary element of existence, it can more easily than anything else rouse and influence the thinking mind.

Schopenhauer

Good literature continually read for pleasure must, let us hope, do some good to the reader: must quicken his perception thought dull, and sharpen his discrimination though blunt, and mellow the rawness of his personal opinions.

Alfred Edward Houseman

Books are good enough in their own way, but they are a mighty bloodless substitute for life.

Stevenson

Read not to contradict and confirm; not to believe and take for granted; not to find talk and discourage; but to weigh and consider. Some books are to be tasted, others to be read, but not curiously; and some few to be read wholly, and with diligence and attention. Reading maketh a full man; conference a ready man; and writing an exact man.

Bacon

Reading is nothing more than a substitute for thought of one's own.

Schopenhauer

Those who have spent their lives in reading, and taken their wisdom from books, are like people who have obtained precise information about a country from the description of many travelers. Such people can tell a great deal about it, but, after all they have not connected, clear, and profound knowledge of its real condition. But those who have spent their lives in thinking, resemble the travelers themselves; they alone really know what they are talking about; they are acquainted with the actual state of affairs, and are quite at home in the subject.

Schopenhauer.

He who is guided by his genius, he who thinks for himself, who thinks spontaneously and exactly, possesses the only compass by which he can steer aright. A man should read only when his own thoughts stagnate at their source, which will happen often enough even with the best of minds. On the other hand, to take up a book for the purpose of scaring away one's own original thoughts is sin against the Holy Spirit.

Schopenhauer

Reading deprives the mind of all elasticity; it is like keeping a spring continually under pressure. The safest way of having no

thoughts of one's own is to take up a book every moment one has nothing else to do.
Schopenhauer

To think with one's own head is always to aim at developing a coherent whole system, even though it be not a strictly complete one; and nothing hinders this so much as to string a current of there thoughts, such as comes of continual reading.
Schopenhauer

There is no better recreation for the mind than the study of the ancient classics. Take any one of them into your hand, be it only for half and hour, and you will feel yourself refreshed, relieved, purified, ennobled, strengthened; just as though you had quenched your thirst at some pure spring. Is this the effect of the old language and its perfect expression, or is it the greatness of the minds whose works remain unharmed and un-weakened by the lapse of a thousand years?
Schopenhauer

The book which you read from a sense of duty, or because for any reason you must, does not commonly make friends with you.
William Dean Howells

A man ought to read just as inclination leads him; for what he reads as a task will do him little good. A young man should read five hours in a day and so may acquire a great deal of knowledge.
Samuel Johnson

I conceive that knowledge of books is the basis on which all other knowledge rests.
George Washington

No matter what his rank or position may be. the lover of books is the richest and happiest of the children of men.
John Alfred Langford

Read the best books first, or you may not have a chance to read them at all.

Henry David Thoreau

That is a good book which is opened with expectation and closed with profit.

Louisa May Alcott

Books are the ever-burning lamps of accumulated wisdom.

George William Curtis

As you grow ready for it, somewhere or other you will find what is needful for you in a book.

George Macdonald

A house without books is like a room without windows.

Horace Mann

Reading is to the mind what exercise is to the body. As by the one, health is preserved, strengthened and invigorated: by the other, virtue (which is the health of the mind) is kept alive, cherished and confirmed.

Joseph Addison

Let us tenderly and kindly cherish.. the means of knowledge. Let us dare to read, think, speak and write.

John Adams

My books have accompanied me all along my way, and assist me everywhere. They comfort me in old age and solitude. They free me from the well of a tedious idleness. and release me at any moment from disagreeable company. Books dull the pangs of any grief that is not intense and overmastering. To distract myself they easily draw my mind to themselves and away from other things.

And yet they show no resentment when they see that I only turn to them through lack of those other more real, likely and natural satisfactions; they always receive me with the same welcome
Montaigne
Montaigne Essays p. 261

It is a great thing to start life with a small number of really good books, which are your very own.
Sir Arthur Conan Coyle

The mind that is over-loaded with alien thought is thus deprived of all clear insight, and is well-nigh disorganized.
Schopenhauer

A scientific thinker has need of much knowledge, and so must read a great deal, his mind is nevertheless strong enough to master it all, to assimilate and incorporate it with the system of his thought, and so to make it fit in with the organic unity of his insight, which, though vast, is always growing. And in the process, his own thought, like the bass in an organ. always dominates everything and is never drowned by the other tones.
Schopenhauer

"We both know that no book is going to change your life. Only you can actually change your life. I can't do it for you. No teacher can."
Harvey Mackay

If you would profit by the experience of others there is no better or more interesting way than to learn from the lives of great men how they overcame their difficulties and made a place for themselves in the world. A good biography will tell you two things about the man; "what and how produced was the effect of society on him, what and how produced was his effect on society." If you know these things, you know the real man; you know what the

advantages and the difficulties of his life and time made of him, and what he, in turn, did for the world.
Macaulay

Poetry ennobles the heart and the eyes, and unveils the meaning of all things upon which the heart and the eyes dwell. It discovers the secret rays of the universe, and restores to us forgotten paradise.
Dame Edith Sitwell.

No entertainment is as cheap as reading, nor any pleasure so lasting.
Lady Mary Wortley Montague.

If I couldn't read, I couldn't live.
Thelma Green.

Reading, after a certain age, diverts the mind too much from its creative pursuits. Any man who reads too much and uses his own brain too little falls into lazy habit of thinking.
Albert Einstein.

Force yourself to reflect on what you read paragraph by paragraph.
Samuel Taylor Coleridge.

It is well to read everything of something, and something of everything.
Lord Brougham.

A page digested is better than a volume hurriedly read.
Thomas Babington Macaulay.

He picked something valuable out of everything he read.
Pliny the Elder.

We read too much; we have forgotten how to listen.

SELF-RESPECT

I've learned
that the important thing
is not what others think of me,
but what I think of me.
    H. Jackson Brown Jr.

The most magnificent cathedrals are not outside you but inside you.
    Albert Schweitzer.

The strongest single factor in prosperity consciousness is self-esteem: Believing you can do it, believing you deserve it, believing you will get it.
    Jerry Gillies

I must be myself. I cannot break myself any longer for you, or you. If you can love me for what I am, we shall be the happier. If you cannot, I will still seek to deserve that you should. I will not hide my tastes or aversions.
    Emerson

Whose would be a man, must be a nonconformist.
    Emerson

Never esteem anything as of advantage to thee that shall make thee break thy word or lose self-respect.
    Marcus Aurelius

Nothing can bring you peace but yourself.
    Emerson

I count him braver who overcomes his desire than him who overcomes his enemies; for the hardest victory is victory over self.
Aristotle

He who attends to his greater self becomes a great man, and he who attends to his smaller self becomes a small man.
Mencius

No bird soars too high, if he soars with his own wings.
William Blake

A liberated woman is one who feels confident in herself, and is happy in what she is doing. She is a person who has a sense of self...It all comes down to freedom of choice.
Betty Ford

Doubt whom you will, but never yourself.
Christian N. Bovee

When we cannot find contentment in ourselves; it is useless to seek it elsewhere.
Francois De La Rochefoucauld

Rest, satisfied with doing well and leave others to talk of you as they please.
Pythagoras.

Self-respect is sometimes the relearning and dropping of old habits. Affirmations are an effective way of changing our habits and goals. "Design your own affirmations. The writer of Mentally Tough suggested, "make it short and simple, and then be thorough about getting the message across to yourself. Use signs, messages, tapes, chants-anything you can think of. Your acquaintances and co-workers will think you're abnormal, and they'll be right; normal people (losers) don't take positive personal action to change their attitudes. It will take time, but the message will eventually soak through to your most innermost emotional recess, changing your attitude and thus your responses and performance.

Dr. James E. Loehr
Peter J. McLaughlin
Mentally Tough p. 57

The following is a list of affirmation suggestions from L.S. Barksdale, The Barksdale Foundation

(Use, memorize, and enjoy those you agree with.)

I accept full responsibility for the consequences of my actions.

I allow myself the freedom to make mistakes, to be wrong," to fail.

I analyze and benefit from my mistakes.

I make my own decision and willingly accept the consequences.

I think for myself and speak and act with deliberation.

I stand up for my own opinion and convictions.

I do not vacillate-I make the best choice I can at the time.

I do not accept condemnation, "put-downs" or insults.

I do not condemn or belittle myself for my mistakes and shortcomings.

I do not blame others for my problems, mistakes, defeats or handicaps.

I take deep satisfaction in doing my work conscientiously and well.

I do not lean on others for unjustified financial or moral support.

I face reality and resist nothing I cannot change.

I refuse to accept condemnation, blame, shame or guilt.

I refrain from no endeavor for fear of unsatisfactory results.

I do not depend on others for reconfirmation or approval.

I do not accept advice against my better judgment.

I am patient, kind and gentle with myself.

I discipline myself in line with my life experience.

I do nothing to excess-I avoid self-indulgence.

I fulfill all commitments both to myself and others.

I follow all undertakings through to a logical conclusion.

I take the initiative in personal contacts and relationships.

I freely express any emotion I see fit.

I readily admit my mistakes and shortcomings.

I walk erect and look everyone in the eye with a friendly gaze.

I do not exaggerate, rationalize, lie or alibi.

I do not allow personal comparisons to affect my self-esteem.

I do not criticize, belittle or condemn others.

I do not demand confirmation and agreement.

I am warm and friendly toward all I contact.

I recognize everyone with consideration and respect.

I feel warm and loving toward myself..

I am authentic, true to my own needs, values, and convictions.

I am invulnerable to the reactions and criticism of others.

I do not indulge in self-pity.

I defer to no one on account of his wealth, power or prestige.

I do not fear others' pronouncements, attitudes and opinions.

I am frank and open with everyone I contact.

I count my blessings and rejoice in my growing awareness.

I make the most of every day of my life.

SOLITUDE

The creative person is constantly seeking to discover himself, to remodel his own identity, and to find meaning in the universe through what he creates. He finds this a valuable integrating process which, like meditation or prayer, has little to do with

other people, but which has its own separate validity. His most significant moments are those in which he attains some new insight, or makes some new discovery; and these moments are chiefly, if not invariably, those in which he is alone.
Anthony Storr

The way to keep from having thoughts of one's own is to constantly focus on someone else's thoughts that have been written for Radio and Television.
R. V.E.

Conversation enriches the understanding, but solitude is the school of genius; and the uniformity of a work demotes the hand of a single artist.
Edward Gibbon

Some development of the capacity to be alone is necessary if the brain is to function at its best, and if the individual is to fulfill his highest potential. Human beings easily become alienated from their own deepest needs and feeling. Learning, thinking, innovation, and maintaining contact with one's own inner world are all facilitated by solitude.
Anthony Storr

Solitude helps people do some solid planning for the future, so they don't just take the events of life as they come.
Father James Gill
Hartford Institute of living

Many psychotherapists consider solitude a basic human need
Anthony Storr
Children that grow up with television, rock music and endless activities, often have an underdeveloped taste for solitude, a very necessary part of life.
Richard B. Clarke
Amherst College

It is the mark of a superior man that left to himself, he is able endlessly to amuse, interest and entertain himself out of his personal stock of meditations, ideas, criticisms, memories, philosophy, humor and what not.
George Jean Nathan.

Until I truly loved I was alone.
Caroline Elizabeth Sarah Norton.

It would do the world good if every man in it would compel himself occasionally to be absolutely alone.

Most of the world's progress has come out of such loneliness.
Bruce Barton.

Solitude shows us what we should be; society shows us what we are.
Richard Cecil.

The strongest man in the world is he who stands most alone.
Henrik Ibsen.

TEACHING

The difference between teaching and learning is dramatic. The excitement of learning what High School students call relevant material is missing. Our schools need to help students individualize their own thinking. Students need to record in their own book, what they think about all the senses they experience: touching, smelling, seeing, hearing.

Their purpose should be to increase their experience and create a personal philosophy. This will multiply their mistakes and develop their enthusiasm for solving problems.

Mistakes should be encouraged in every way possible. They are the best possible source of experience, happiness, and eventually wisdom. Mistakes are education in disguise, they should be considered a positive chance to test and exercise courage.

Creativity is the backbone, heart and soul of self-fulfillment. All of life's creativity must pass through the tips-of-our-fingers. Writing is a record, and proof the student is actively involved in his or her own learning process. Those who design their own education find more of life's pleasure. They are in control of their success and are more willing to accept responsibility for their failures.

R. V.E.

Everyone is a teacher: parent or friend, manager or owner, artist or musician, apprentice or master craftsman. We have an obligation to share what we know with what we do not know No bubble is so iridescent or floats longer than that blown by the successful teacher.

William Osler

Who supplies another with a constructive thought has enriched him forever.

Alfred A.Moniapert

The best way to gain from the success of a hero is to admire it, for what we admire we unconsciously emulate.

Teaching children can be compared with training a racehorse. They must be disciplined so they do not run off the track, but too much discipline will take away the fighting spirit that makes the race so much fun.

Students don't become problems for teachers. Teachers become problems for students that get in the way of the teachers objectives. The whole art of teaching is only the art of awaking the natural curiosity of young minds.

Anatole France

Not he is great who can alter matter, but he who can alter my state of mind.

Emerson

Everything in our world has it's own particular nature. What ever goes up must come down. Waves in the ocean continue endlessly. Plants, animals and people have natural tendencies. Students with relevant problems wish to learn, want to grow, seek to discover, endeavor to master, desire to create and move toward self-discipline. Successful teachers know Mother Nature.

If I distrust the human being then I must cram him with information of my own choosing. lest he go his own mistaken way. But if I trust the capacity of the human individual for developing his own potentiality, then I can provide him with many opportunities and Permit him to choose his own way and his own learning direction.

Carl Rogers

Stupidity and confused mind are not to be cured by a word of admonition; and we may fitly say of this kind of correction that Cyrus replied to one who urged him to harangue his army when on the point of entering into battle. "That men are not suddenly made brave and warlike by a fine harangue, any more than a man immediately becomes a musician after hearing a good song." It needs a preliminary apprenticeship, A long and continued education.

Montaigne

To Be what we are, and to become what we are capable of becoming, is the only end of life

Stevenson

The best cure for a sluggish mind is to disturb it's routine.
William H. Danforth

Jean Piaget said, "Every time we teach a child something we keep him from inventing it himself." I would go a step further. Every time we teach a child something. rather that helping: him learn, we keep him from inventing himself. By its very nature, teaching homogenizes, both its subjects and its objects. Learning on the other hand, liberates. The more we know about ourselves and our world, the freer we are to achieve everything we are capable of achieving.
Warren Bennis
On Becoming a Leader. 70

Too often we give children answers to remember, rather than problems to solve.
Roger Lewin

We are all teachers at sometime in our life; mother, father, doctor, lawyer, manager. Someone said that the teacher often learns more than the student. I suppose the reason is the teacher is usually out numbered and may pick up ideas that are varied, both in subject and style. A teacher is an individual who by association collects thoughts and feelings that are individual in them-selves. Association with other human beings is a learning situation, regardless of their age or background.

A teacher, because of their position, either at the head of the class, or an executive in the front office must make an attempt to be a good role model. Students often learn more from watching how you act, than from listening to the words you speak. There are many ways to teach, but in a situation where students are able to watch your activities; you can be sure they will imitate how you act rather than listening to your words.

Because of this your action must follow the activity of your mind or you will be discovered as a phony or less than an honest person. Truth follows you around where ever you go. So if your intention is that of a teacher, sincerity is a must. Your patience, courtesy, and good manners all effect what kind of person your student will be at a later age.

R. V.E.

The one exclusive sign of a thorough knowledge is the power of teaching.

Aristotle.

Let our teaching be full of ideas. Hitherto it has been stuffed only with facts.

Anatole France.

The true aim of every one who aspires to be a teacher should be, not to impart his own opinions, but to kindle minds.

Frederick William Robertson.

THINKING

"It makes no difference to me what you think of me. The only thing that matters to me, is what I think of you."

This above comment is the statement of, supposedly, a person who has a high self esteem. It could also be the statement of an egomaniac. Most everyone agrees that it would be foolish to try and please everyone. So, I think having good or acceptable manners and respect for others helps us fit in with those we associate with. It's a good idea to be sensitive to other people problems and wishes. But if we become too sensitive we become weak and very much like everyone else. We need to be true to ourselves. We are stronger if we live, "who we are," not what some one thinks we should be.

Socrates said, the most important thing we can do for ourselves is "know-thyself." I think it is a good idea to look at ourselves, see what we are good at and do everything we can to maximize the use of our own ability. We always have more potential than we are using.

R. V.E.

The ability to doubt is
uncommon, and is found only
among educated persons.
Aristotle

Do not under any circumstance ignore the thoughts that are going through your head. Listen to yourself and pay attention. Record your thoughts and use them in a productive way. They are important. Find some way to convince your self that what you think is important to both yourself and the world you live in. Being convinced will improve your world. It will change and improve how you feel about yourself. It is easy to become so engrossed with the mere mechanics of business as to lose the habit of thought. Easy to say, "Yours received and contents noted" a certain number of times during the day, and go home with the notion that one has done a good day's work. When the really valuable work of the day could have been and should have been done under the shower in the morning, or in the fifteen-minute walk across the park to the office.

T.S. Elliot in Ash Wednesday said,
"Teach us to sit still." He is echoing
Pascal's comment that most of the
     world's ills were chargeable to the fact
that not enough men are attached to their
    chairs. What Elliot and Pascal
 bemoaned, of course, was the decline of
contemplation.
Norman Cousins

The body travels more easily than the mind, and until we have limbered up our imagination we continue to think as though we had stayed home. We have not really budged a step until we take up residence in someone else's point of view.
John Erskine.

Reading and learning are things that anyone can do of his own free will; but not so thinking. Thinking must be kindled, like a fire by a draught; it must be sustained by some interest in the matter in hand. When a man thinks for himself, he follows the impulse of his own mind, which is determined for him at the time, either by environment or some particular recollection.
Schopenhauer

What this power is, I cannot say; all I know is that it exists and it becomes available only when a man is in that state of mind in which he knows exactly what he wants and is fully determined not to quit until he finds it.
Alexander Graham Bell

The works of all truly capable minds are distinguished by a character of decision and definiteness, which means they are clear and free from obscurity. A truly capable mind always knows definitely and clearly what it is that it wants to express, whether its medium is prose, verse, or music.
Schopenhauer

Everyone who really thinks for himself is so far like a monarch. His position is un-delegated and supreme. His judgments, like royal decrees, spring from his own sovereign power and proceed directly from himself. He acknowledges authority as little as a monarch admits a command; he subscribes to nothing but what he has himself authorized.

Schopenhauer

Cherish your vision and your dreams as they are the children of your soul; the blue prints of your ultimate achievements.

Napoleon Hill

Men and women must think, and must feel themselves free to think. The lowest misery is slavery, not of the body, but of thought. Even when our life is harsh and heroic destiny provided we maintain the invincibility of the mind.

Gilbert Highet

Thinking, Learning, remembering, knowing; imagining and creating new ideas; preserving and communicating knowledge over distances in time and space. Not only is it wonderful in its compass and variety; it is unique. It makes us human.

Gilbert Highet

The life of every individual man and woman is made up of many acts and passions. But it is most clearly and consistently seen as a pattern of learning. We think all the time. Our thoughts and our experiences continually form a mass of material, which we accept and try to organize. It is chiefly in the depth and completeness of its organization that we differ from one another.

Gilbert Highet

A wise man of our own time was once asked what was the single greatest contribution of Greece to the world's welfare. He replied "The greatest invention of the Greeks was to think," "on the one hand and the other hand." Without these two balances, we cannot think.

Gilbert Highet

One of the truest saying of the medieval thinkers was, "All things pass into calculate, but also to wonder; to admire; to expect the unexpected

Gilbert Highet

Yes, the outer world-both visible and invisible- is ultimately a mystery. So too is the other world we inhabit-the inner world, the world of the mind. Not one of us knows what his own mind contains. Not one of us knows what his own mind can do, or will produce.

Gilbert Highet

Truth that has been merely learned is like an artificial limb, a false tooth, a waxen nose; at best, like a nose made out of another's flesh; it adheres to us only because it is put on. But truly acquired by thinking of our own is like a natural limb; it alone really belongs to us. This is the fundamental difference between the thinker and the mere man of learning. The intellectual attainments of a man who thinks for himself resemble a fine painting, where the light and shade are correct, the tone sustained, the color perfectly harmonized; it is true to life. On the other hand, the intellectual attainments of the mere man of learning are likely systematically arranged, but devoid of harmony, connection and meaning.

Arthur Schopenhauer

We can do only what we think we can do. We can be only what we think we can be. We can have only what we think we can have. What we do, what we are, what we have, all depend upon what we think.

Robert Collier

It is a privilege to learn to use his own mind rather than just somebody else's mind.
Howard Lowry

It is not a matter of surprise that a man who thinks for himself can easily be distinguished from the book-philosopher by the very way in which he talks, by his marked earnestness, and the originality, directness, and personal conviction that stamp all his thoughts and expressions.
Schopenhauer

Intellectual blemishes, like facial ones, grow more prominent with age.
La Rochefoucauld

No problem can stand the assault of sustained thinking.
Voltaire

If you wish to be agreeable, you must pretend to be taught many things you already know.

Whether you think you can or think you can't -you are right.
Henry Ford

A man is literally what he thinks.
James Allen

Opinions then that are opposed to mine do not offend or estrange me; they only arouse and exercise my mind. When a man opposes me he arouses my attention, not my anger. I meet him half-way if he contradicts and corrects me. The cause of truth ought to be the cause common to both of us. I hail and welcome the truth in whatever hand I find it,

I cheerfully surrender and tender my vanquished sword to her, as soon as I see her approach in the distance.
Montaigne

What the mind of man can conceive and believe, the mind of man can achieve.
Napoleon Hill

Nurture your mind with great thoughts; to believe in the heroic makes heroes.
Benjamin Disraeli

He can who thinks he can, and he can't who thinks he can't. This is an inexorable, indisputable law.
Orison Swett Marden

Man's mind, once stretched by a new idea, never regains it's original dimensions.
Oliver Wendell Holmes

The mind is a strange machine, which can combine the materials offered to it in the most astonishing ways, but without materials from the external world it is powerless
Bertrand Russell

A man can always sit down and read, but not-think. It is with thoughts as with men; they cannot always be summoned at pleasure; we must wait for them to come. Thought about a subject must appear of itself, by a happy and harmonious combination of external stimulus with mental temper and attention; and it is this that which never seems to come to people.
Schopenhauer

A scientific thinker has need of much knowledge, and so must read a great deal, his mind of nevertheless strong enough to master it all, to assimilate and incorporate it with the system of his thought, and so to make it fit in with the organic unity if his insight, which, though vast, is always growing. And in the process, his own thought, like the bass in an organ, always dominates everything and is never drowned by the other tones.

Schopenhauer

He who is guided by his genius, he who thinks for himself, who thinks spontaneously and exactly, possesses the only compass by which he can steer aright. A man should read only when his own thoughts stagnate at their source, which will happen often enough even with the best of minds. On the other hand, to take up a book for the purposes of scaring away one's own original thoughts is sin against the Holy Spirit.

Schopenhauer

A man may have a great mass of knowledge, but if he has not worked it up by thinking it over for himself, it has much less value than a far smaller amount which he has thoroughly pondered ; for it is only when a man looks at his knowledge from all sides, and combines the things he knows by comparing truth with truth, that he obtains a complete hold over it and gets it in to his power. A man cannot turn over anything in his mind unless he knows it; he should therefore, learn something; but it is only when he has turned it over that he can be said to know it.

Schopenhauer

No one will ever succeed in doing anything really great and original in the way of thought, which does not seek to acquire knowledge for him, and, making this the immediate object of his studies.

Schopenhauer

All that is good in man lies in youthful feeling and mature thought.

Joseph Joubert

Give your thoughts the respect they deserve by writing them down. Good thoughts are no better than good dreams, unless they are executed.
Everson

The key to every man is his thought.
Everson

Learning to really think requires first that we make room for it by diminishing the domain of feelings.
Reuven Bar-Levav M.D.

Don't worry about what people think about you, because they aren't thinking about you.

Man is complex being full of contradictions between thinking and feeling.
Reuven Bar-Levav M.D.

Very few of our race can be said to be yet finished men.
Emerson.,

Thinking is an instrument within experience.
Thinking is a tool of science.
Thinking is not life; it is a tool of life.
Joseph H Hart

The thinking person is likely to distrust feelings, and the feeling person tends to distrust facts and logic.
James L. Adams

Every person whose mind has not been subdued by the drill of school education has a natural curiosity inflamed by the living and thinking of other men.
Emerson

Negative emotions lead away from performance and directly to sloppy thinking and inappropriate responses. You face tremendous social pressures to do what they're doing, to think as they think, to fit in-to, be an also-ran. When you have a positive attitude, you seldom respond the way that everyone else responds. We find it hard to believe that other people's thoughts are as silly as our own, but they probably are.

James H. Robinson

Congratulate him or her. They are probably doing the company a lot more good than anything else they could be doing. They're thinking. It's the hardest, most valuable task any person performs. It's what helped get you there. THINK: it's the one-word motto of the most imitated company in the country. I.B.M.

Harvey Mackey

The presence of a thought is like the presence of a woman we love. We fancy we shall never forget the thought nor become indifferent to the dear one. But out of sight out of mind! The finest thought runs the risk of being irrevocably forgotten if we do not write it down. and the darling of being deserted if we do not marry her.

Schopenhauer
The Art of literature P 53

We cultivate the mind. We are lovers of the beautiful, simple in our tastes, without loss of manliness.

Thucydides

Wise men think out their thoughts; fools proclaim them.
Heinrich Heine.

CHAPTER 14

QUOTATIONS

TRUTH

No legacy is so rich as honesty
William Shakespeare

To measure the man measure his heart.
Malcolm S. Forbes

Rather fail with honor than succeed by fraud.
Sophocles

You cannot do wrong without suffering wrong.
Everson

It is better to deserve honors and not have them than to have them and not deserve them
Mark Twain

Understand this law and you will then know, beyond room for the slightest doubt, that you are constantly punishing yourself for every wrong you commit and rewarding yourself for every act of constructive conduct in which you indulge.

Napoleon Hill

Honesty is the first chapter in the book of wisdom.
Thomas Jefferson

The greatest homage we can pay to truth is to use it.
Emerson.

What we have in us of the image of God is the love of truth and justice.
Domosthenes.

I have always found that the honest truth of our own mind has a certain attraction for every other mind that loves truth honestly.
Thomas Carlyle.

If it is the truth what does it matter who says it.
Anonymous.

Facts that are not frankly faced have a habit of stabbing us in the back.
Sir Harold Bowden.

When in doubt, tell the truth.
Mark Twain

Let us then be what we are, and speak what we think, and in all things keep ourselves loyal to truth.
Henry Wadsworth Longfellow

Truth is a deep kindness that teaches us to be content in our everday life and share with the people the same happiness.
Kahlil Gibran.

A man who seeks truth and loves it must be reckoned precious to any human society.
Frederick The Great.

WISDOM

All that is good in man lies in youthful feeling and mature thought.
Joseph Joubert

Though a man be wise; it is no shame for him to live and learn.
Sophocles

Do not trust those in whom the compulsion to punish is strong.
Nietzsche

Science gives us knowledge, but only philosophy can give us wisdom.
Will Durant

Knowledge without wisdom is a load of books on the back of an ass.
Japanese Proverb

Many receive advice, only the wise profit from it.
Syrus

An empty man is full of himself.
Edward Abbey

He must be a wise man who knows what is wise.
Xenophon

The fool wonders, the wise man asks.
Benjamin Disraeli

The trouble with people is not that they don't know but that they know so much that ain't so.
Josh Billings

Wisdom is only good for today. Tomorrow will require a new judgment or thought. Wisdom is only good at the moment of its use. There are only a few bits of wisdom that are ageless.

The most manifest sign of wisdom is a constant happiness.
Schopenhauer

Man really knows nothing save what he has learned by his own experience.
Christopher M. Wieland

Yesterday is a canceled check;
tomorrow is a promissory note;
today is the only cash you have,
so spend it wisely.
Kay Lyons

A single conversation across the table with a wise man is worth a month's study of books.
Chinese Proverb

A mans education on earth, it seems to be agreed, is concerned primarily with his search for "the good life." It is easier to see the good life working in people than to say what it is. Those who have it are guided unassumingly by the copybook virtues of moderation, kindliness, and charity. They face tragic situations with dignity and courage; they are realistic, adaptable, and outgoing , by which I mean that they wish well to others and help when they can without parade or fuss. They give more than they receive, but don't worry about it. They haven't a trace of goody-goodiness; they usually have humor.

They are the healthy who live by love.
Wilmarth Sheldon Lewis
One Man 's Education p. 488

The more we study, the more we discover our ignorance.
Percy Shelley

Most people find wisdom where they look. Some never look. Wisdom lies in the recognition of your own ignorance.
Socrates

A wise man does not put all of his eggs in one basket
Ancient proverb

Your greatest discovery is to discover your true self.

Your greatest adventure is to accept the ancient challenge laid down by Socrates: Know-Thyself.

Your greatest step toward wisdom is the ability to read your own heart. Dennis Dierot reminds us: "when we know how to read our own hearts. We acquire wisdom of the hearts of others." Before you can read your own heart, however, you must first ask yourself these ten questions: what am I? Who am I? Why am I? What do I really believe? For what and for whom do I live? What are my highest loyalties? What is my primary purpose, my one most important goal? What is my responsibility to the Present and to the Future?

In your search to discover yourself, you are wise to identify and destroy whatever masks you might have been wearing. "We are so much accustomed to disguising ourselves to other," Rochefoucauld reminds us, "that at length disguise ourselves, to ourselves."

In that search to discover yourself, you are wise to be painfully honest with yourself. "Do not shelter the mirror which reflects your soul's lack of beauty," advised Jean Nicholas Grou. "Rather welcome the truth, and believe that next to the knowledge of God nothing is so precious as the knowledge of self."

William Arthur Ward
Quote Magazine
Sept 9-1979 p. 198

Those who are wise, think they are wise, but their hunger for wisdom is never satisfied   your search for wisdom is a search for the genius that is inside of you. It's what Socrates called Know-thyself. An important lifetime goal is find your own individual wisdom. It's Gods gift to you. No one else has what you have. Your search must be intentional, "those who search find."

A man in the gold-rush day was asking how he found so much gold. His answer was, " I dig more." We become what our thoughts are. Wisdom is not accidental; it is the result of living with your eyes wide open.

R. V.E.

My belief is that to have no wants is devine.
Socrates

The beginning of wisdom is the definition if terms.
Socrates

WORK

A man doesn't learn to understand anything unless he loves it.

Goethe

Genius is one percent inspiration and ninety-nine percent perspiration.
Thomas Edison

Don't wait for your ship to come in, swim out to it.

A book salesman tried to sell a farmer a set of books on agriculture, explaining to the farmer, "you could farm twice as good as you do now" the farmer replied, "Listen, young fellow I ain't farming half as good as I know how now."

To love what you do and feel that it matters-how could anything be more fun?
Katharine Graham

Luck is what happens when preparation meets opportunity.
Letterman

I've only worked half days, all of my life. My advice to you is to do the same. It doesn't matter which half..., the first twelve hours or the second twelve hours.
Harvey Mackay

The reward of a thing well done is to have do it.
Ralph Waldo Emerson.

Few things are impossible to diligence and skill. Great works are performed not by strength, but perseverance.
Samuel Johnson

He conquers who endures.
Persius

People forget how fast you did a job, but they remember how well you did it.
Howard W. Newton

Expecting high performance from ourselves means that we are not afraid of work, that we enjoy it, and that if things don't go right we will find another way.
R. V.E.

All great works or achievements require time.
David Joseph Schwartz

A working man sure of his skills goes leisurely about his job and accomplishes much though he works as if at play.
Eric Hoffer
The ordeal of Change. p. 2

Whatever you can do or dream you can, begin it.
Goethe

The only person who saves time is the one who spends it wisely. Self respect and a measure of success in work as well as a sense of concern and compassion for others is a widely held middle class view. Through work one gains self- respect and the ability to control, at least in part, one's environment.
Habit of the Heart   p. 204

Most people agree that connectedness to others in work, love, and community is essential to happiness, self-esteem, and moral worth.
Habits of the Heart. p. 84

The more intelligent you are, the more idleness irks you. Some people succeed by great talent, some by the influence of friends, some by a miracle. But. the majority succeed by hard work.
Eleanor Roosevelt

I try all things; I achieve what I can.
Herman Melville

I would rather be sick than idle.
Seneca

When Demosthenes was asked what was the first part of oratory, he answered , "Action:" and which was the second, he replied, "action;" and which was the third, he still answered, "Action."
Plutarch

Verily, when the Day of Judgment comes, we shall not be asked what we have read, but what we have done.
Thomas A. Kempis

It is difficult to retain the knowledge one has acquired, without putting it into practice.
Pliny Younger

Everywhere in life, the true question is not what we gain, but what we do.
Thomas Carlyle

Lord, grant that I may always desire more than I can accomplish.
Michelangelo

Ambition and love are the wings of great actions.
Goethe

I never work better than when I am inspired by anger. When I am angry I can write, pray, and preach well; for them my whole temperament is quickened, my understanding sharpened, and all mundane vexations and temptations depart.
Martin Luther

Our grand business undoubtedly is, not to see what lies dimly at a distance, but do what lies clearly at hand.
Thomas Carlyle Huxley

WRITING

Any writer overwhelmingly honest about pleasing himself is almost sure to please others.
Marianne Moore.

My purpose is to entertain myself first and other people secondly.
John D. Macdonald.

I write in order to attain that feeling of tension relieved and function achieved which a cow enjoys on giving milk.
H.L. Mencken.

Anything that is written to please the author is worthless.
Blaise Pascal.

Your audience is one single reader. I have found that sometimes it helps to pick out one person-a real person you know, or an imagined person and write to that one.
John Steinbeck.

A kid is a guy I never wrote down to. He's interested in what I say if I make it interesting. He is also the last container of a sense of humor, which disappears as he gets older, and he laughs only according to the way the boss, society, politics, or race want him to. Then he becomes an adult. An adult is an obsolete child.
Theordore Geisel (Dr. Seuss.)

In a very real sense, the writer writes in order to teach himself, to understand himself, to satisfy himself.
Alfred Kazin.

To write is to write is to write is to write is to write is to write. is to write is to write.
Gertrude Stein.

A poet never takes notes. You never take notes in a love affair.
Robert Frost.

My stories have led me through my life. They shout I follow. They run up and bite me on the leg-I respond by writing down everything that goes on during the bite. When I finish, the idea lets go, and runs off.
Ray Bradbury.

When I want to read a good book, I write one.
Benjamin Disraeli.

It is better to do the wrong thing than to do nothing.
Winston Churchill

There are three rules for writing a novel. Unfortunately, no one knows what they are.
Somerset Maughham.

A single sentence in your writing might revolutionize someone's life.
Cecil Murphey

The good expositor should choose key works and play upon them.
Henry James

To write is to be naïve, and one of the strange pleasures of writing is the discovery that one has said aloud what other people are saying silently.
Edmund Bergler, M.D..

The writer is more deeply involved than the average person, while a certain part is totally detached! And it is that part that observes, gains a comprehensive view of a situation, makes implications, identifies problems, and begins reaching for solutions.
Ruth Vaughn

Putting pen to paper lights more fire than matches ever will.
Malcolm Forbes.

Clear prose indicates the absence of thought.
Marshall McLean.

The way Bernard Shaw believes in himself is very refreshing in these atheistic days when so many believe in no God at all.
Israel Agnail.

I'm not an author, but before I became mayor, I wasn't a mayor.
Edward Koch.

I was a writing fool when I was eleven years old and have been tapering off ever since.
E.B. White.

Teaching has ruined more American novelists than drink.
Gore Vidal

Talent alone cannot make a writer. There must be a man behind the book.
Ralph Waldo Emerson.

Books are the quietest and most constant of friends...and the most patient of teachers.

Charles W. Eliot.

Any man who will look into his heart and honestly write, what he sees there, will find plenty of readers.

Edgar Watson Howe.

The writer must be willing, above everything else, to take chances, to risk making a fool of himself-or even to risk revealing the fact that he is a fool.

Jessamyn West.

A man should never be ashamed to own he has been in the wrong, which is but saying in other words that he is wiser to-day than he was yesterday.

Alexander Pope.

SUMMARY

My summary in ten words or less; why we suffer so much pain in every community, worldwide.

- Lack of leadership in schools and prisons.
- Students need focused freedom one hour each day.
- Prison inmates must educate-themselves eight hours a day.
- We must learn what risk, action and courage can teach us.

Education is a cure for most of our societies ills. Our education problems can be corrected by improving focus on the natural interest and enthusiasm students have. Education can be improved with the simple use of freedom for only one hour each day. Students need the freedom to follow their curiosity. If they take no risks with their ability to think for themselves, and if they do not have the right and the courage to make mistakes, they will be disappointed in themselves. When this happens all kinds of unusual attitude and habits take their place. They will need a gang that accepts them as they are. Lack of self-discipline and lazy habits do not take them to the excellence they deserve and can achieve. Young people need a challenge so they" learn how to learn." They need the freedom to learn from their own mistakes. Adults need to loosen their desire to control with the simple process of facilitation of what students are interested in. Children naturally gravitate to what could be called "Liberal Education;" but students are stifled by "controlling" adults who dogmatically see back to basics-education as the only solution.

Basics are necessary, but a small window of freedom each day can dramatically improve the "will to learn," both at home and in school. If we want quality control or if we want to evaluate our education system we should take a serious look at what our problems are, and what the cause is. When a manufacturer of a product has a flaw they usually examine the product in every way possible.

The flawed products of our society are hidden in a warehouse of decay; our prisons. (Out of sight out of mind.) Education has not been fun for these young people. This, if you think about it, is rather strange. Strange because I don't think we can deny, everyone enjoys learning. The problem is we force students to learn the way we think they should learn; so we are only fooling ourselves if we insist on teaching them the way they "don't want to learn." We are constantly fighting an uphill battle. I have to say, "what fools we are! Our cost of manufacture and waste is tremendous. The business of "education" is not a profitable business for us to invest money in. I suggest we need a new C.E.O..... If we examine any highly successful business, (for investment purposes) we look for leadership.

Most strong leaders have a passion, which interrupts their sleep at night. Their passion, in fact, their obsession is to find a need and fill that need in a way that no one else can touch. In other words they are competitive to a point of obsession for "service" to their client. They set the pace and allow no one to give better service. We must ask ourselves, do our children deserve passionate leadership that can see the need and fill the need? We all know, this is not even a question!

Management of any situation can be improved with the study of leadership through Management Consultants. There are many who suggest we make changes. Three of the best are:

Dr. Carl R.Rogers. "Students who have Freedom are enthusiastic students.

Dr. Peter Drucker. "We must maximize the use of three words: time, space, and material."

Dr W. Edwards Deming "School administrators and teachers must share, equally, responsibility or success."

OUR SCHOOLS AND PRISONS HAVE
IDENTICAL PROBLEMS

THEY DENY NATURAL LEADERSHIP POSSIBILITIES
AND DO NOT ENCOURAGE PERSONAL GROWTH.

"THEY OVER-MANAGE"

We have a choice and a decision we must make. We can
physically punish prison inmates every hour of every day in
many ways. We can bitterly and hatefully get even with them
for all of the pain they have caused us, or we can change who
they have been and who they are with facilitation of change in
their habits and thinking. I see no profit in creating uneducated
animals that will eventually be our neighbors. In fact, I believe
if we look in the mirror we will see who is responsible. Old-
timers like myself have created schools that do not work. Self-
education is our only answer. If we want our life too improve we
must provide leadership. How can we be so foolish to think that
throwing money at the problem will help? Did Abraham Lincoln
and so many others have expensive schools and teachers? Let's be
realistic; a passionate desire to get the job done, the right attitude
has more value than all the money in the world.

If we want peace in our communities we must have peace in
our prisons. We are in my opinion "pretty damn" weak Manager's
if we can't teach an inmate who wants to learn and has the time.
I've heard people say, "You must have Cancer to understand
Cancer. I emphatically disagree. Cancer can be devastating. Our
prisons are the cancer of our society. Do you need prison time to
believe it? I hope not!
The only way to find peace in our prisons is to open up the
floodgates of personal interest, curiosity and the desire to learn.
The freedom to learn will help inmates find their own self-
designed wisdom. They want to become a whole man, mentally
and physically. This is a goal they will willingly work hard to
achieve, but they want to do it their way or not at all.

They have had enough of schools that force them to learn in a way they cannot and do not want to learn. If we treat them like they are all fools, they will live up to our expectations, and return to our communities, fools. But, there are very few inmates who cannot learn to be civilized citizens.

Those who cannot can be easily separated and confined. Classification is very simple: Their social skills and attitude will separate the men from the boys. They accept and actually want tough decisions; the last thing they want is to be pampered by anyone.

"Our prisons can work successfully if they imitate our economic system." I often think, how is it possible our society works with people running around in different directions, each with a different purpose. There is one line that runs through everyone's thinking; they want freedom to manage their own time. They want to be who they want to be without interference. Everyone has a goal, and freedom clearly stands out above all other goals.

What would happen if everyone had to stay in their own little community. "It's the law." Lack of free interaction with each other would prevent the possibility of each of us learning from each other. Wisdom can be found in almost every situation, but because of prison management personal growth is not possible.

My point is, inmates must have the opportunity to learn how to fit into their communities. An empty, self-centered brain has no community value, so their work--as you and I must work--should focus on intellectual change. A prison manager's only purpose is re-education on the inside of an outside perimeter fence.

Self-education has no taxpayer cost; in fact operation cost's can be dramatically reduced when inmate thinking has been refocused. Most human beings have the ability to change, grow and get better with time.

Absolute control is wrong if it defeats the purpose.

Inmate cooperation, with each other, can raise the level of thinking, without destroying what they believe to be, "individualism." We must begin where cooperation is possible and allow it to grow in every possible way. If in-mates do not change their thinking and habits, taxpayers are not getting their money's worth. Prison should be a positive experience for our communities; a Win/Win situation for taxpayers, inmates and prison managers. We have a right to demand change. We should tolerate nothing less. A partial and practical solution is for us to realize and believe (Rather than denial.) that our largest, MANAGEABLE--CONTROLABLE, source of crime comes directly from our prison system. That may be difficult to believe because most people don't realize that a prison is only a temporary warehouse for bodies.

Most of these young men and women, we must not forget, will soon be our neighbors. The cure: Inmates should work eight hours each day like all of us are expected to do. There job is very simple, it is Self-Education, and it is their responsibility not that of the tax payers. Their focus should be entirely on personal growth. The muscle between their ears is the only muscle that needs their attention. Leadership in prisons very much like that in our schools have a tendency to OVER MANAGE, rather than make use of a natural flow of human curiosity and enthusiasm.

If we cannot convince ourselves learning is fun and easy when students are responsible for part of it themselves, our prisons and crime will continue to grow.

A manager's only work is to fill that need. What is that old aphorism "You can lead a horse to water, but you can't make them drink." I suggest if inmates don't want to drink, they can have "a cot and three meals a day" for the rest of their life.

Our communities have only one responsibility; that is to see that inmates have this "water to drink." It is NOT being done! This great water, this sea of knowledge, is not available in any prison I know of. Education has not been made important in our prisons.

Taxpayers are clearly being "ripped off" by managers who keep their job as simple as possible. Few CIVIL SERVICE MANAGERS enjoy a good challenge. Rather than do a job that obviously needs to be done, they let themselves off easy. Why should they build a new path when we are allowed to follow the same old rut they have always been in? It is absolutely true, if we want something different than we are getting, we need to do something different than what we are doing.

We need a leader who has the courage to climb to the top of the trees and point out what our direction should be. Almost no parolees are ready for the "streets" yet nearly all prison inmates return to their communities. Inmates have the ability to learn, but when they went to jail they had few social skills. Sadly, they have even less when they leave the prison because of the environment that does not challenge or change them in any way.

SELF-DESIGNED EDUCATION

It seems the world is constantly changing, and so is our thinking. There is however, in my opinion, one truth that will never change. "You will always benefit from what you give without expecting something in return." A gift freely given, with no strings attached, will improve the quality of your life. Truly, what goes around comes around.

We are all teachers in some way, like it or not, our activities are constantly being watched by our young people. There are a thousand ways to teach, so it's our duty to learn "how best to teach" with the special skills that only we have. No one else can teach the way "you can" so you need to find our own style; what works best for you.

Since we are all different, we should learn from and celebrate that difference. We can learn by reading, but action created by writing turns our thoughts into a more useful, effective self-designed education.

Writing creates a purpose for reading, and reading creates a purpose for writing. This cyclical effect becomes a whirlpool of learning. Simplicity at it's best. You will get back what you put "into" it.

About the Author

Richard Eastman as a teenager lived a life that few could imagine. He finished only half of the seventh grade and none of the eighth grade. He left home at the age of fourteen. Later as a Youth Counselor he claimed to be the "Worlds Best Listener."

Richard believes "Learning" is an adventure if you invent and design your own class. He thinks if students wait for a teacher to teach, their education will be a disaster. Emerson said, "Most people live in quiet desperation." Life without the excitement of learning becomes one television show after another. Teenagers must have at least one-hour each day to write a script of their own show...their own life.

Printed in the United States
46349LVS00001B/7